AMERICA'S HEALTHY COOKING

salads

AMERICA'S HEALTHY COOKING

salads

JG
PRESS

Published by World Publications Group, Inc.
455 Somerset Avenue
North Dighton, MA 02764
www.wrldpub.net

All photographs courtesy of Sunset Books

ISBN 1-57215-414-4

Editors: Joel Carino and Emily Zelner
Designer: Lynne Yeamans/Lync
Production Director: Ellen Milionis

Printed and bound in China by SNP Leefung Printers Limited.

1 2 3 4 5   06 05 03 02

salads

melon, papaya & cucumber salad

preparation time: about 25 minutes

3 small cantaloupes

1 medium-size firm-ripe papaya, peeled, seeded, and diced

1 medium-size cucumber, peeled, seeded, and diced

About 2 tablespoons minced fresh mint or 1 teaspoon dried mint, or to taste

3 tablespoons lime juice

1 tablespoon honey

Mint sprigs

1 Cut 2 of the melons in half lengthwise. Scoop out and discard seeds. If a melon half does not sit steadily, cut a very thin slice from the base so the melon half does sit steadily. Set melon halves aside.

2 Peel, seed, and dice remaining melon. Transfer to a large nonmetal bowl. Add papaya, cucumber, minced mint, lime juice, and honey. Mix gently to combine.

3 Set a melon half in each of 4 bowls (or on each of 4 dinner plates). Spoon a fourth of the fruit mixture into each melon half. (At this point, you may cover and refrigerate for up to 4 hours.) Just before serving, garnish each melon half with mint sprigs.

makes 4 servings

per serving: 135 calories, 3 g protein, 33 g carbohydrates, 0.8 g total fat, 0 mg cholesterol, 28 mg sodium

red & yellow pepper salad

preparation time: about 25 minutes

5 large yellow bell peppers

1 large red bell pepper, seeded and diced

^{2}/$_3$ cup peeled, minced jicama

2 tablespoons minced cilantro

1 ^{1}/$_2$ tablespoons distilled white vinegar

1 teaspoon honey

About ^{1}/$_8$ teaspoon ground red pepper (cayenne), or to taste

1 Set 4 of the yellow bell peppers upright, then cut off the top quarter of each. Remove and discard seeds from pepper shells; set shells aside. Cut out and discard stems from top pieces of peppers; then dice these pieces and transfer to a large nonmetal bowl.

2 Seed and dice remaining yellow bell pepper and add to bowl. Then add red bell pepper, jicama, cilantro, vinegar, honey, and ground red pepper; mix gently.

3 Spoon pepper mixture equally into pepper shells. (At this point, you may cover and refrigerate salad for up to 4 hours.).

makes 4 servings

per serving: 90 calories, 3 g protein, 21 g carbohydrates, 0.6 g total fat, 0 mg cholesterol, 7 mg sodium

warm chinese chicken salad

preparation time: about 25 minutes

1/3 cup seasoned rice vinegar (or 1/3 cup distilled white vinegar plus 2 teaspoons sugar)

1 tablespoon reduced-sodium soy sauce

1 1/2 teaspoons sugar

1 1/2 teaspoons Asian sesame oil

7 cups (about 7 oz.) finely shredded iceberg lettuce

3 cups (about 3 oz.) bite-size pieces of radicchio

1/3 cup lightly packed cilantro leaves

1/4 cup sliced green onions

1 pound skinless, boneless chicken breast, cut into thin strips

2 cloves garlic, minced or pressed

Cilantro sprigs

1 In a small bowl, stir together vinegar, 1 tablespoon water, soy sauce, sugar, and oil; set aside.

2 In a large serving bowl, combine lettuce, radicchio, cilantro leaves, and onions; cover and set aside.

3 In a wide nonstick frying pan or wok, combine chicken, 1 tablespoon water, and garlic. Stir-fry over medium-high heat until chicken is no longer pink in center; cut to test (3 to 4 minutes). Add water, 1 tablespoon at a time, if pan appears dry. Add vinegar mixture to pan and bring to a boil. Quickly pour chicken and sauce over greens, then mix gently but thoroughly. Garnish with cilantro sprigs and serve immediately.

makes 4 servings

per serving: 185 calories, 28 g protein, 10 g carbohydrates, 3 g total fat, 66 mg cholesterol, 626 mg sodium

nectarine, plum & basil salad-salsa

preparation time: under 20 minutes

2 large firm-ripe nectarines, pitted and diced

2 large firm-ripe plums, pitted and diced

1/4 cup firmly packed fresh basil leaves (minced) or about 1 tablespoon dried basil, or to taste

1 1/2 tablespoons red wine vinegar

1 tablespoon honey

4 to 8 large butter lettuce leaves, rinsed and crisped

1 In a large nonmetal bowl, mix nectarines, plums, basil, vinegar, and honey. (At this point, you may cover and refrigerate for up to 4 hours.)

2 To serve, place 1 or 2 lettuce leaves on each of 4 dinner plates. Spoon a fourth of the fruit mixture onto each plate.

makes 4 servings

per serving: 83 calories, 1 g protein, 20 g carbohydrates, 0.7 g total fat, 0 mg cholesterol, 2 mg sodium

warm spinach, pear & sausage salad

preparation time: about 30 minutes

3 green onions

8 ounces spinach, stems removed, leaves rinsed and crisped

1 large yellow or red bell pepper, seeded and cut lengthwise into thin strips

5 medium-size firm-ripe pears

1 teaspoon olive oil or vegetable oil

8 to 10 ounces mild or hot turkey Italian sausages, casings removed

$^1/_3$ cup balsamic vinegar

$^3/_4$ teaspoon fennel seeds

1 Trim and discard ends of onions. Cut onions into 2-inch lengths; then cut each piece lengthwise into slivers. Tear spinach into bite-size pieces. Place onions, spinach, and bell pepper in a large serving bowl, cover, and set aside.

2 Peel and core pears; slice thinly. Heat oil in a wide nonstick frying pan or wok over medium-high heat. When oil is hot, add pears and stir-fry until almost tender to bite (about 5 minutes). Lift pears from pan with a slotted spoon; transfer to a bowl and keep warm.

3 Crumble sausage into pan and stir-fry over medium-high heat until browned (5 to 7 minutes); add water, 1 tablespoon at a time, if pan appears dry. Add pears, vinegar, and fennel seeds to pan. Stir gently to mix, scraping browned bits free from pan bottom. Immediately pour hot pear mixture over spinach mixture; toss gently but thoroughly until spinach is slightly wilted.

makes 4 servings

per serving: 155 calories, 3 g protein, 36 g carbohydrates, 2 g total fat, 0 mg cholesterol, 36 mg sodium

cucumber & green onion salad

preparation time: about 40 minutes

3 cucumbers, thinly sliced

1 tablespoon salt

$^1/_2$ cup thinly sliced green onions

$^1/_3$ cup seasoned rice vinegar; or $^1/_3$ cup distilled white vinegar plus 2 $^1/_2$ teaspoons sugar

1 tablespoon sugar

Pepper

1 In a bowl, lightly crush cucumbers and salt with your hands. Let stand for 20 to 30 minutes; then turn into a colander, squeeze gently, and let drain. Rinse with cool water, squeeze gently, and drain well again. (At this point, you may cover and refrigerate until next day)

2 In a nonmetal bowl, mix cucumbers, onions, vinegar, and sugar. Season to taste with pepper. Serve in bowl or transfer with a slotted spoon to a platter. Serve cold or at room temperature.

makes 8 servings

per serving: 38 calories, 1 g protein, 9 g carbohydrates, 0.2 g total fat, 0 mg cholesterol, 337 mg sodium

stir-fried pork & escarole salad

preparation time: about 30 minutes

3 quarts lightly packed rinsed, crisped escarole or spinach leaves

²/₃ cup cider vinegar

3 tablespoons honey

2 large Red Delicious apples, cored and thinly sliced

4 teaspoons cornstarch

1 cup fat-free reduced-sodium chicken broth

2 teaspoons Dijon mustard

¹/₂ teaspoon dried thyme

2 teaspoons olive oil

2 large shallots, chopped

1 pound lean boneless pork loin, loin end, or leg, trimmed of fat and cut into paper-thin ¹/₂- by 3-inch slices

1 cup raisins

1 Place escarole on a wide serving platter. In a medium-size bowl, stir together vinegar, honey, and apples. Then remove apples with a slotted spoon and scatter over escarole. Add cornstarch, broth, mustard, and thyme to vinegar mixture in bowl; stir well and set aside.

2 Heat oil in a wide nonstick frying pan or wok over medium-high heat. When oil is hot, add shallots and pork and stir-fry until meat is lightly browned (about 3 minutes). Push meat to one side of pan. Stir vinegar mixture well, pour into pan, and stir just until boiling (about 1 minute). Stir meat into sauce; then quickly spoon meat mixture over escarole and sprinkle with raisins.

makes 4 servings

per serving: 443 calories, 28 g protein, 67 g carbohydrates, 9 g total fat, 67 mg cholesterol, 305 mg sodium

watercress, butter lettuce & shrimp salad

preparation time: about 35 minutes

1 tablespoon mustard seeds

¹/₄ cup boiling water

Olive oil cooking spray

2 ¹/₂ cups ¹/₂-inch cubes sourdough French bread

¹/₄ cup balsamic or red wine vinegar

2 teaspoons Dijon mustard

1 tablespoon olive oil

2 ¹/₂ quarts torn butter lettuce leaves, rinsed and crisped

2 ¹/₂ quarts lightly packed watercress sprigs, rinsed and crisped

8 ounces small cooked shrimp

1 Place mustard seeds in a small bowl; pour boiling water over them. Let stand for at least 10 minutes or up to 8 hours; drain well.

2 Spray a shallow rimmed baking pan with cooking spray. Spread bread cubes in pan; spray with cooking spray. Bake in a 350° oven until crisp and golden brown (12 to 15 minutes). Let cool in pan on a rack. (At this point, you may store airtight at room temperature for up to 2 days.)

3 In a small bowl, stir together mustard seeds, vinegar, mustard, and oil. Arrange lettuce, watercress, and shrimp in a large salad bowl; add mustard seed dressing and mix lightly until greens are coated. Top salad with croutons.

makes 6 servings

per serving: 123 calories, 12 g protein, 10 g carbohydrates, 4 g total fat, 74 mg cholesterol, 229 mg sodium

litchi, penne & chicken salad

preparation time: about 40 minutes

5 ounces (about 1 1/2 cups) dried penne

1 can (about 11 oz.) litchis

3/4 cup plain low-fat yogurt

3/4 teaspoon grated lemon peel

4 teaspoons lemon juice

1 1/2 teaspoons dried thyme

2 cups bite-size pieces cooked chicken

1/2 cup finely diced celery

8 large butter lettuce leaves, rinsed and crisped

1/3 cup chopped green onions

Salt and pepper

1 Bring 8 cups water to a boil in a 4- to 5-quart pan over medium-high heat. Stir in pasta and cook just until tender to bite (8 to 10 minutes); or cook according to package directions. Drain, rinse with cold water until cool, and drain well.

2 Drain litchis, reserving 1/3 cup of the syrup; set fruit aside. In a large nonmetal bowl, mix reserved 1/3 cup litchi syrup, yogurt, lemon peel, lemon juice, and thyme. Add pasta, chicken, and celery. Mix thoroughly but gently. (At this point, you may cover pasta mixture and fruit separately and refrigerate for up to 4 hours; stir pasta occasionally.)

3 Arrange lettuce on individual plates. Top with pasta mixture and litchis. Sprinkle with onions. Offer salt and pepper to add to taste.

makes 4 servings

per serving: 358 calories, 28 g protein, 47 g carbohydrates, 7 g total fat, 65 mg cholesterol, 136 mg sodium

roasted bell pepper & black bean salad

preparation time: about 25 minutes

2 large red bell peppers

1/2 cup seasoned rice vinegar; or 1/2 cup distilled white vinegar plus 1 tablespoon sugar

1 tablespoon olive oil

1 tablespoon honey

1/2 teaspoon chili oil

3 cans (about 15 oz. *each*) black beans, drained and rinsed; or 6 cups cooked (about 3 cups dried) black beans, drained and rinsed

1/4 cup minced cilantro

2 tablespoons thinly sliced green onion

Salt

Cilantro sprigs

1 Cut peppers in half lengthwise. Set pepper halves, cut side down, in a 10- by 15-inch rimmed baking pan. Broil 4 to 6 inches below heat until charred all over (about 8 minutes). Cover with foil and let cool in pan. Then remove and discard skins, stems, and seeds; cut peppers into strips or chunks.

2 In a bowl, mix vinegar, 1 tablespoon water, olive oil, honey, and chili oil. Add beans and roasted peppers; mix gently but thoroughly. (At this point, you may cover and refrigerate until next day.)

3 To serve, stir minced cilantro and green onion into bean mixture. Season to taste with salt and garnish with some cilantro sprigs.

makes 6 servings

per serving: 295 calories, 16 g protein, 52 g carbohydrates, 4 g total fat, 0 mg cholesterol, 400 mg sodium

kidney cobb salad

preparation time: about 25 minutes

DRESSING:

1/3 cup non-fat mayonnaise

1/3 cup nonfat sour cream

2 tablespoons balsamic vinegar

2 tablespoons smooth unsweetened applesauce

1 tablespoon olive oil

1 tablespoon Dijon mustard

1 tablespoon chopped fresh dill or 1 teaspoon
   dried dill weed

1 teaspoon sugar, or to taste

Dill sprigs (optional)

SALAD:

2 cans (about 15 oz. *each*) red kidney beans

1 large yellow or red bell pepper

6 ounces feta cheese

1 very small red onion

1 large head red leaf lettuce, separated into
   leaves, rinsed, and crisped

1 package (about 10 oz.) frozen tiny peas,
   thawed and drained

1 For dressing, in a small bowl, combine mayonnaise, sour cream, vinegar, applesauce, oil, mustard, chopped dill, and sugar. Beat until smoothly blended. If a thinner dressing is desired, add water, 1 tablespoon at a time, until dressing has the desired consistency. Spoon into a small serving bowl; garnish with dill sprigs, if desired. Cover lightly and refrigerate while you prepare salad.

2 Drain beans and rinse well. Seed and finely chop bell pepper. Crumble cheese. Thinly slice onion; separate slices into rings.

3 To assemble salad, line a rimmed platter or a wide salad bowl with large lettuce leaves, then break remaining leaves into bite-size pieces and arrange atop whole leaves. Mound peas, beans, bell pepper, and cheese separately on lettuce; place onion in center. Offer dressing to add to taste.

makes 6 servings

per serving: 256 calories, 16 g protein, 32 g carbohydrates, 7 g total fat, 25 mg cholesterol, 718 mg sodium

ginger oil

preparation time: about 10 minutes

1/4 cup ground ginger

1 cup vegetable oil or olive oil

1 In a small pan, whisk together ginger and 1/4 cup of the oil until well blended. Gradually whisk in remaining 3/4 cup oil. Heat over medium heat, stirring often, just until warm (not hot or boiling). Remove from heat and let cool slightly.

2 Carefully pour oil into a clean, dry glass bottle or jar, leaving ginger sediment behind; discard sediment. (Or strain oil, if desired.) Cover airtight and store for up to 6 months.

makes about 1 cup

per tablespoon: 124 calories, 0.1 g protein, 1 g carbohydrates, 14 g total fat, 0 mg cholesterol, 0.4 mg sodium

split pea & green pea salad

preparation time: about 45 minutes

1 cup green split peas

2 cups vegetable broth

1/2 teaspoon dried thyme

1 package (about 10 oz.) frozen tiny peas (do not thaw)

4 ounces (about 10 tablespoons) dried orzo or other rice-shaped pasta

1/4 cup thinly sliced green onions

1/4 cup chopped fresh mint

1/4 cup vegetable oil

1 teaspoon finely shredded lemon peel

2 tablespoons lemon juice

About 24 large butter lettuce leaves, rinsed and crisped

Mint sprigs

Thyme sprigs

Salt and pepper

1 Sort through split peas, discarding any debris; then rinse and drain peas. In a 1 ½- to 2-quart pan, bring broth to a boil over high heat. Add split peas and dried thyme. Reduce heat, cover, and simmer until split peas are tender to bite (about 25 minutes); drain and discard any remaining cooking liquid. Transfer split peas to a large bowl, add frozen peas, and mix gently but thoroughly. Let stand, stirring occasionally, until mixture is cool (about 3 minutes).

2 Meanwhile, in a 4- to 5-quart pan, bring about 8 cups water to a boil over medium-high heat; stir in pasta and cook until just tender to bite, about 5 minutes. (Or cook pasta according to package directions.) Drain, rinse with cold water, and drain well again. Transfer pasta to bowl with peas. Add onions and chopped mint; mix gently. In a small bowl, beat oil, lemon peel, and lemon juice until blended. Add to pea mixture; mix gently but thoroughly.

3 To serve, line 4 individual plates with lettuce leaves; top each plate equally with pea mixture. Garnish salads with mint and thyme sprigs. Season to taste with salt and pepper.

makes 4 servings

per serving: 458 calories, 19 g protein, 62 g carbohydrates, 15 g total fat, 0 mg cholesterol, 607 mg sodium

cilantro slaw

preparation time: about 15 minutes

8 ounces green cabbage, very finely shredded (about 3 cups)

8 ounces red cabbage, very finely shredded (about 3 cups)

1 cup firmly packed cilantro leaves, minced

1/4 cup lime juice

1 tablespoon *each* water and honey

1/2 teaspoon cumin seeds

Salt and pepper

In a large nonmetal bowl, mix green cabbage, red cabbage, cilantro, lime juice, water, honey, and cumin seeds. Season to taste with salt and pepper. If made ahead, cover and refrigerate for up to 4 hours.

makes 6 servings

per serving: 33 calories, 1 g protein, 8 g carbohydrates, 0.2 g total fat, 0 mg cholesterol, 14 mg sodium

fruited quinoa salad

preparation time: about 45 minutes

2 tablespoons pine nuts or slivered almonds

1 1/4 cups dried apricots

1 1/2 cups quinoa or 1 cup bulgur

2 teaspoons olive oil or vegetable oil

2 or 3 cups fat-free reduced-sodium chicken broth

2 teaspoons grated lemon peel

2 tablespoons lemon juice

1 cup dried currants

Salt

1 Toast pine nuts in a small frying pan over medium heat until golden brown (3 to 5 minutes), stirring often. Transfer nuts to a bowl; set aside. Coarsely chop 1/2 cup of the apricots; set aside.

2 Place quinoa in a fine strainer; rinse thoroughly with water (bulgur needs no rinsing). Heat oil in a 3- to 4-quart pan over medium heat. Add quinoa or bulgur; cook, stirring often, until grain turns a slightly darker brown (8 to 10 minutes).

3 To pan, add broth (3 cups for quinoa, 2 cups for bulgur), lemon peel, and lemon juice. Bring to a boil over high heat. Reduce heat, cover, and simmer until grain is just tender to bite (10 to 15 minutes). Drain and discard any liquid from grain. Stir chopped apricots and 1/2 cup of the currants into grain. Let stand until warm; or let cool, then cover and refrigerate until next day.

4 To serve, season quinoa mixture to taste with salt. Mound mixture in center of a serving dish or large rimmed serving platter. Garnish with remaining 3/4 cup apricots, remaining 1/2 cup currants, and pine nuts.

Makes 6 servings.

per serving: 349 calories, 10 g protein, 70 g carbohydrates, 7 g total fat, 0 mg cholesterol, 81 mg sodium

wilted spinach salad with oranges

preparation time: about 35 minutes

2 medium-size oranges

2 quarts lightly packed spinach leaves, rinsed and crisped

1 large onion, thinly sliced and separated into rings

1/4 cup balsamic or red wine vinegar

2 teaspoons vegetable oil

1 teaspoon dried tarragon

1 Grate 1 teaspoon peel (colored part only) from one of the oranges; set aside. With a sharp knife, cut remaining peel and all white membrane from both oranges. Holding fruit over a bowl to catch juice, cut between membranes to free segments; place segments in bowl with juice and set aside. Place spinach in a large salad bowl.

2 In a wide frying pan, combine onion, vinegar, oil, tarragon, and grated orange peel. Place over medium-low heat, cover, and cook until onions are tender-crisp when pierced (6 to 8 minutes). Gently stir in orange segments and juice. Pour orange mixture over spinach. Mix lightly, then serve at once.

makes 4 servings

per serving: 103 calories, 4 g protein, 18 g carbohydrates, 3 g total fat, 0 mg cholesterol, 70 mg sodium

black bean & jicama salad

preparation time: under 20 minutes

1 can (about 15 oz.) black beans, drained and rinsed; or 2 cups cooked (about 1 cup dried) black beans, drained and rinsed

1 cup peeled, finely chopped jicama

1/4 cup crumbled panela or feta cheese

3 tablespoons lime juice

1/3 cup minced cilantro

2 tablespoons thinly sliced green onion

2 teaspoons honey

1/4 teaspoon crushed red pepper flakes

4 to 8 butter lettuce leaves, rinsed and crisped

1 In a bowl, combine beans, jicama, cheese, lime juice, cilantro, onion, honey, and red pepper flakes. Mix well. (At this point, you may cover and refrigerate for up to 4 hours.)

2 To serve, spoon bean mixture into lettuce leaves.

makes 4 servings

per serving: 164 calories, 9 g protein, 28 g carbohydrates, 2 g total fat, 8 mg cholesterol, 100 mg sodium

mizuna, fennel & crab salad

preparation time: under 20 minutes

12 ounces fennel

2/3 pound mizuna, bare stems trimmed, leaves rinsed and crisped

2/3 cup plain nonfat yogurt

1/4 cup reduced-fat sour cream

2 tablespoons lemon juice

1 tablespoon Dijon mustard

1 teaspoon dried tarragon

1/2 teaspoon sugar

1 1/2 pounds cooked crabmeat

1 Cut feathery tops from fennel; chop tops and set aside for dressing. Cut root ends and any bruised spots from fennel head; then thinly slice (you should have 2 cups) and place in a large bowl.

2 Reserve 3/4 cup of the mizuna for dressing. Cut remaining mizuna into 2- to 3-inch long pieces; add to bowl with fennel.

3 To prepare dressing, in a blender or food processor, combine the 3/4 cup reserved mizuna, yogurt, sour cream, lemon juice, mustard, 1 tablespoon of the reserved chopped fennel tops, tarragon, and sugar. Whirl until puréed; set aside.

4 Mound crab on mizuna mixture, placing the most attractive crab pieces on top. At the table, add dressing to salad; mix gently.

makes 6 servings

per serving: 172 calories, 27 g protein, 7 g carbohydrates, 4 g total fat, 117 mg cholesterol, 460 mg sodium

white bean & tomato salad

preparation time: about 1 1/2 hours

1 large red onion, cut into 3/4-inch chunks

2 1/2 teaspoons olive oil

2 tablespoons balsamic or red wine vinegar

12 to 14 medium-size firm-ripe pear-shaped (Roma-type) tomatoes, cut lengthwise into halves

Salt

3 cans (about 15 oz. *each*) cannellini (white kidney beans)

2 tablespoons *each* chopped fresh thyme and chopped fresh basil; or 2 teaspoons *each* dry thyme and dry basil

Pepper

1 In a lightly oiled square 8- to 10-inch baking pan, mix onion, 1/2 teaspoon of the oil, and vinegar. Arrange tomatoes, cut side up, in a lightly oiled 9- by 13-inch baking pan; rub with remaining 2 teaspoons oil, then sprinkle with salt.

2 Bake onion and tomatoes in a 475° oven until edges of onion chunks and tomato halves are dark brown (40 to 50 minutes for onion, about 1 hour and 10 minutes for tomatoes); switch positions of baking pans halfway through baking.

3 Pour beans and their liquid into a 2- to 3-quart pan. Add fresh thyme (or both dry thyme and dry basil). Bring to a boil; reduce heat and simmer for 3 minutes, stirring. Pour beans into a fine strainer set over a bowl; reserve liquid. Place beans in a serving bowl; tap herbs from strainer into beans.

4 Chop 8 tomato halves; stir into beans along with fresh basil (if used) and onion. Add some of the reserved liquid to moisten, if desired. Season to taste with salt and pepper. Arrange remaining 16 to 20 tomato halves around edge of salad.

makes 8 side dish or 4 main-dish servings

per serving: 179 calories, 10 g protein, 32 g carbohydrates, 2 g total fat, 0 mg cholesterol, 566 mg sodium

autumn pear salad

preparation time: 20 minutes

1/4 cup red wine vinegar

2 tablespoons extra virgin olive oil

1 tablespoon drained capers

1 tablespoon lemon juice

1/4 teaspoon *each* pepper and honey

4 large firm-ripe red pears

1 package prewashed spinach leaves, coarse stems and any yellow or bruised leaves discarded, remaining leaves rinsed and crisped

8 ounces mushrooms, thinly sliced

3/4 cup dried cranberries

4 ounces sliced pancetta or bacon, crisply cooked, drained, and crumbled

1 In a large bowl, combine vinegar, oil, capers, lemon juice, pepper, and honey; beat until well blended. Set aside.

2 Core pears and cut each into about 16 wedges. As pears are cut, transfer them to bowl with dressing; mix gently to coat with dressing. Add spinach, mushrooms, and cranberries; mix until coated with dressing. Then divide salad among individual plates and sprinkle with pancetta.

makes 8 servings

per serving: 160 calories, 3 g protein, 27 g carbohydrates, 6 g total fat, 5 mg cholesterol, 163 mg sodium

warm cioppino salad

preparation time: about 30 minutes

1/4 cup lemon juice

1 teaspoon dried basil

1 teaspoon dried oregano

2 cloves garlic, minced or pressed

3 quarts lightly packed rinsed, crisped spinach leaves, torn into bite-size pieces

1 tablespoon olive oil

8 ounces extra-large raw shrimp (26 to 30 per lb.), shelled and deveined

2 cups thinly sliced mushrooms

2 cups thinly sliced zucchini

1 can (about 14 1/2 oz.) tomatoes, drained and chopped

12 pitted ripe olives

8 ounces cooked crabmeat

1 To prepare lemon dressing, in a small bowl, stir together lemon juice, basil, oregano, and garlic; set aside.

2 Place spinach in a wide serving bowl, cover, and set aside.

3 Heat oil in a wide nonstick frying pan or wok over medium-high heat. When oil is hot, add shrimp and stir-fry until just opaque in center; cut to test (3 to 4 minutes). Remove from pan with tongs or a slotted spoon and set aside.

4 Add mushrooms and zucchini to pan; stir-fry until zucchini is just tender to bite (about 3 minutes). Return shrimp to pan; add tomatoes, olives, and lemon dressing. Stir until mixture is heated through. Pour shrimp mixture over spinach, top with crab, and mix gently but thoroughly.

makes 6 servings

per serving: 149 calories, 18 g protein, 10 g carbohydrates, 15 g total fat, 85 mg cholesterol, 380 mg sodium

tomatillo & tomato salad

preparation time: about 15 minutes

3 pounds (about 10 cups) ripe cherry tomatoes (red, yellow, yellow-green, orange); include some that are 1/2 inch or less in diameter

10 medium-size tomatillos, husked, rinsed, and thinly sliced

1 fresh jalapeño chile, seeded and minced

1/2 cup lightly packed cilantro leaves

1/4 cup lime juice

Salt and pepper

Lime wedges

1 Cut any tomatoes larger than 3/4 inch in diameter into halves; then place tomatoes in a nonmetal bowl.

2 Add tomatillos, chile, cilantro, and lime juice; mix gently. Season to taste with salt and pepper; serve with lime wedges.

makes 8 to 10 servings

per serving: 39 calories, 2 g protein, 8 g carbohydrates, 0.6 g total fat, 0 mg cholesterol, 14 mg sodium

PREPARING SALAD GREENS: Putting salads together is simpler if you rinse and crisp the greens in advance (up to a few days before use). Each time you make a tossed salad, try to prepare several meals' worth of greens. First discard the coarse outer leaves and stems; then rinse the remaining leaves and dry them in a lettuce spinner (or drain on paper towels or a clean dishtowel). Wrap the leaves loosely in dry paper towels; store in a plastic bag in the crisper of your refrigerator. When you're ready for salad, your greens will be clean, chilled, and crisp. You can even store salad ready-made: just fill plastic bags with torn greens and crisp vegetables such as sliced radishes, celery, and bell pepper.

asian salad

preparation time: about 40 minutes

6 cups lightly packed rinsed, crisped spinach leaves

¼ cup unseasoned rice vinegar or white wine vinegar

2 tablespoons reduced-sodium soy sauce

2 teaspoons honey

1 teaspoon Asian sesame oil

2 teaspoons sesame seeds

2 teaspoons vegetable oil

5 cups broccoli flowerets

1 pound carrots, cut into ¼-inch diagonal slices

1½ cups thinly sliced celery

1 medium-size onion, thinly sliced

1 Arrange spinach leaves on a large platter; cover and set aside. In a small bowl, stir together vinegar, soy sauce, honey, and sesame oil; set aside.

2 In a wide nonstick frying pan or wok, stir sesame seeds over medium heat until golden (about 3 minutes). Pour out of pan and set aside. Heat 1 teaspoon of the vegetable oil in pan over medium-high heat. When oil is hot, add half of the broccoli, carrots, celery, and onion. Stir-fry until vegetables are hot and bright in color (about 3 minutes). Add ⅓ cup water to pan, cover, and cook until vegetables are just tender to bite (about 3 minutes). Uncover and continue to cook, stirring, until liquid has evaporated (1 to 2 more minutes). Remove vegetables from pan and set aside. Repeat to cook remaining broccoli, carrots, celery, and onion, using remaining 1 teaspoon vegetable oil and adding ⅓ cup water after the first 3 minutes of cooking.

3 Return all cooked vegetables to pan and stir in vinegar mixture. Spoon vegetables onto spinach-lined platter and sprinkle with sesame seeds.

makes 6 servings

per serving: 118 calories, 6 g protein, 20 g carbohydrates, 3 g total fat, 0 mg cholesterol, 297 mg sodium

hot chile oil

preparation time: about 10 minutes

6 to 12 small dried hot red chiles (use the greater number of chiles for more heat)

1 cup vegetable oil or olive oil

1 Place 3 whole chiles in a small pan; add oil. Split each of the remaining 3 to 9 chiles in half; add to pan. Heat over medium heat, stirring gently, just until warm (not hot or boiling). Remove from heat and let cool slightly.

2 With a slotted spoon, remove split chiles and seeds from oil; discard. Remove whole chiles; set aside. Carefully (watch that you don't splatter) pour oil into a clean, dry glass bottle or jar. (Or strain oil, if desired.) Add whole chiles to bottle; cover airtight and store for up to 6 months.

makes about 1 cup

per tablespoon: 121 calories, 0.1 g protein, 0.4 g carbohydrates, 14 g total fat, 0 mg cholesterol, 0.2 mg sodium

shrimp & spinach slaw

preparation time: about 25 minutes

4 cups finely shredded green cabbage

3 cups thinly sliced spinach leaves

1 medium-size cucumber, peeled and sliced

2 medium-size celery stalks, sliced

²/₃ cup plain nonfat yogurt

3 tablespoons reduced-calorie mayonnaise

¹/₂ cup thinly sliced green onions

1 teaspoon grated lemon peel

2 tablespoons lemon juice

1 tablespoon sugar

About 12 large spinach leaves, rinsed and
    crisped (optional)

³/₄ to 1 pound small cooked shrimp

Lemon wedges

Salt and pepper

1 To prepare salad, in a large bowl, combine cabbage, sliced spinach leaves, cucumber, and celery.

2 To prepare yogurt-lemon dressing, in a small bowl, combine yogurt, mayonnaise, onions, lemon peel, lemon juice, and sugar. (At this point, you may cover and refrigerate the salad and dressing separately until next day.)

3 Add dressing to salad and mix well. If using large spinach leaves, use them to garnish salad in bowl; or arrange them around rim of a large platter and mound salad in center. Sprinkle shrimp over salad. Offer lemon wedges to squeeze over salad to taste; season to taste with salt and pepper.

makes 8 servings

per serving: 107 calories, 13 g protein, 9 g carbohydrates, 3 g total fat, 100 mg cholesterol, 189 mg sodium

red slaw

preparation time: 15 minutes

1 medium-size head red cabbage

3 tablespoons *each* balsamic vinegar and salad oil

2 cans (about 15 oz. *each*) red kidney beans,
    drained and rinsed

1 can (about 15 oz.) pickled beets, drained and
    coarsely chopped

2 tablespoons finely chopped crystallized ginger

2 ¹/₂ cups pitted sweet cherries, fresh or
    thawed frozen

1 Remove 4 to 8 large outer cabbage leaves and set aside. Then core cabbage and finely shred enough of it to make 5 cups; set aside. Reserve any remaining cabbage for other uses.

2 In a large bowl, beat vinegar and oil until blended. Stir in beans, beets, and ginger. Gently mix in shredded cabbage and cherries. (At this point, you may cover and refrigerate slaw and whole cabbage leaves separately for up to 4 hours.)

3 To serve, stir sliced onions into slaw. Arrange 1 or 2 of the whole cabbage leaves on each of 4 individual plates. Divide slaw equally among plates; garnish with whole green onions, if desired. Season to taste with salt and pepper.

makes 4 servings

per serving: 468 calories, 16 g protein, 13 g total fat, 78 g carbohydrates, 0 mg cholesterol, 577 mg sodium

mixed greens with pesto dressing

preparation time: 35 minutes

1 tablespoon pine nuts

2 teaspoons Asian sesame oil

1 clove garlic, minced or pressed

3 slices Italian or sourdough sandwich bread, cut into $1/2$-inch cubes

$1/4$ cup chopped fresh basil

$1/4$ cup chopped Italian or regular parsley

1 cup nonfat sour cream

1 tablespoon white wine vinegar

1 teaspoon honey

1 or 2 cloves garlic, peeled

Salt and pepper

8 ounces (about 8 cups) mixed salad greens, rinsed and crisped

1 Toast pine nuts in a wide nonstick frying pan over medium heat until golden (about 3 minutes), stirring often. Pour out of pan and set aside. In same pan (with pan off heat), combine 1 teaspoon of the oil, garlic, and 1 tablespoon water. Add bread cubes and toss gently to coat. Place pan over medium heat; cook, stirring occasionally, until croutons are crisp and tinged with brown (about 10 minutes). Remove from pan and set aside.

2 In a food processor or blender, combine basil, parsley, sour cream, vinegar, honey, remaining 1 teaspoon oil, and garlic; whirl until smoothly puréed. Season to taste with salt and pepper; set aside.

3 Place greens in a large bowl; add dressing and mix gently but thoroughly Add croutons and mix again. Sprinkle with pine nuts.

makes 4 servings

per serving: 154 calories, 8 g protein, 20 g carbohydrates, 4 g total fat, 0 mg cholesterol, 177 mg sodium

fennel & orange salad

preparation time: 20 minutes

2 large heads fennel

$1/4$ cup seasoned rice vinegar

2 tablespoons olive oil

1 tablespoon grated orange peel

1 teaspoon anise seeds

4 large oranges

Seeds from 1 pomegranate

Salt

1 Trim stems from fennel, reserving the feathery green leaves. Trim and discard any bruised areas from fennel; then cut each fennel head into thin slivers. Place slivered fennel in a large bowl.

2 Finely chop enough of the fennel leaves to make 1 tablespoon (reserve remaining leaves); add to bowl along with vinegar, oil, orange peel, and anise seeds. Mix well.

3 Cut off and discard peel and all white membrane from oranges. Cut fruit crosswise into slices about $1/4$ inch thick; discard seeds.

4 Divide fennel mixture among individual plates. Arrange oranges alongside fennel mixture; sprinkle salads equally with pomegranate seeds. Garnish with reserved fennel leaves. Season to taste with salt.

makes 6 servings

per serving: 147 calories, 2 g protein, 26 g carbohydrates, 5 g total fat, 0 mg cholesterol, 290 mg sodium

garbanzo antipasto salad

preparation time: about 50 minutes
chilling time: at least 1 hour

8 ounces sourdough bread, cut into about 1/2-inch cubes

1/2 cup white wine vinegar

2 tablespoons olive oil

1 tablespoon chopped fresh oregano or 1 teaspoon dried oregano

2 teaspoons honey (or to taste)

2 cloves garlic, minced or pressed

1/8 to 1/4 teaspoon pepper

2 cans (about 15 oz. *each*) garbanzo beans, drained and rinsed

2 large tomatoes, chopped and drained well

1/4 cup slivered red onion, in about 1-inch lengths

1/4 cup oil-cured olives, pitted and sliced

3 to 4 tablespoons drained capers

1/3 cup *each* nonfat mayonnaise and nonfat sour cream

2 tablespoons chopped fresh dill or 2 teaspoons dried dill weed

8 to 12 butter lettuce leaves, rinsed and crisped

1 Spread bread cubes in a single layer in a shallow 10- by 15-inch baking pan. Bake in a 325° oven, stirring occasionally, until crisp and tinged with brown (15 to 20 minutes). Set aside. If made ahead, let cool completely in pan on a rack, then store airtight for up to 2 days.

2 In a large bowl, combine vinegar, oil, oregano, honey, garlic, and pepper. Beat until blended. Add beans, tomatoes, onion, olives, and capers; mix gently but thoroughly. Cover and refrigerate for at least 1 hour or up to 4 hours.

3 Meanwhile, in a small bowl, beat mayonnaise, sour cream, and dill until smoothly blended; cover and refrigerate.

4 To serve, line 4 individual rimmed plates or shallow bowls with lettuce leaves. Add croutons to salad and mix gently but thoroughly, being sure to coat croutons with marinade. Then, using a slotted spoon, transfer salad to plates; top each serving with a dollop of dill dressing.

makes 4 servings

per serving: 466 calories, 16 g protein, 67 g carbohydrates, 15 g total fat, 0 mg cholesterol, 1,234 mg sodium

green chile dressing

preparation time: about 10 minutes

1 small can (about 4 oz.) diced green chiles

1/3 cup lime juice

1/4 cup water

1/4 cup chopped cilantro

1 clove garlic, peeled

1 or 2 fresh jalapeño chiles, seeded and chopped

1 1/2 teaspoons sugar

In a blender or food processor, combine green chiles, lime juice, water, cilantro, garlic, jalapeño chiles, and sugar; whirl until smoothly puréed. (At this point, you may cover and refrigerate dressing for up to 4 hours.)

makes about 1 cup

per tablespoon: 5 calories, 0.1 g protein, 1 g carbohydrates, 0.01 g total fat, 0 mg cholesterol, 44 mg sodium

pesto pasta salad

preparation time: 35 minutes

1 cup dried tomatoes (not packed in oil)

2 tablespoons pine nuts

1 pound dried medium-size pasta shells or
    elbow macaroni

1 cup firmly packed chopped fresh spinach

3 tablespoons dried basil

1 or 2 cloves garlic, peeled

1/3 cup grated Parmesan cheese

1/4 cup olive oil

1 teaspoon Asian sesame oil

Salt and pepper

1 Place tomatoes in a small bowl and add boiling water to cover. Let stand until soft (about 10 minutes), stirring occasionally. Drain well; gently squeeze out excess liquid. Cut tomatoes into thin slivers and set aside.

2 While tomatoes are soaking, toast pine nuts in a small frying pan over medium heat until golden (about 3 minutes), stirring often. Pour out of pan and set aside.

3 In a 6- to 8-quart pan, bring 4 quarts water to a boil over medium-high heat; stir in pasta and cook until just tender to bite, 8 to 10 minutes. (Or cook pasta according to package directions.) Drain, rinse with cold water until cool, and drain well again. Pour into a large serving bowl.

4 In a food processor or blender, whirl spinach, basil, garlic, cheese, olive oil, sesame oil, and 1 teaspoon water until smoothly puréed; scrape sides of container as needed and add a little more water if pesto is too thick.

5 Add tomatoes and spinach pesto to pasta; mix well. Sprinkle with pine nuts; season to taste with salt and pepper.

makes 8 servings

per serving: 332 calories, 11 g protein, 49 g carbohydrates, 10 g total fat, 3 mg cholesterol, 78 mg sodium

capellini chinese style

preparation time: about 35 minutes
chilling time: at least 30 minutes

3 tablespoons seasoned rice vinegar; or
    3 tablespoons distilled white vinegar and
    2 teaspoons sugar

3 tablespoons lime juice

4 teaspoons Asian sesame oil (or to taste)

1 tablespoon reduced-sodium soy sauce

1/16 teaspoon ground red pepper (cayenne)

8 ounces dried capellini

1/2 cup thinly sliced green onions

1/3 cup chopped red bell pepper

Lime wedges

1 Combine vinegar, lime juice, oil, soy sauce, and ground red pepper in a large nonmetal serving bowl; mix until blended. Set aside.

2 Bring 8 cups water to a boil in a 4- to 5-quart pan over medium-high heat. Stir in pasta and cook just until tender to bite (about 4 minutes); or cook according to package directions. Drain, rinse with cold water until cool, and drain well.

3 Add pasta to vinegar mixture. Mix thoroughly but gently. Cover and refrigerate until cool (at least 30 minutes) or for up to 4 hours; stir occasionally.

4 Stir in onions and bell pepper just before serving. Offer lime wedges to add to taste.

makes 4 to 6 servings

per serving: 217 calories, 6 g protein, 38 g carbohydrates, 4 g total fat, 0 mg cholesterol, 305 mg sodium

cool beans & bows

preparation time: about 30 minutes
chilling time: at least 30 minutes

4 ounces (about 2 cups) dried farfalle

1/2 cup seasoned rice vinegar; or 1/2 cup distilled white vinegar and 4 teaspoons sugar

1/4 cup minced parsley

1 tablespoon each olive oil, water, and honey

1/4 teaspoon chili oil

1 can (about 15 oz.) kidney beans, drained and rinsed

1 can (about 15 oz.) black beans, drained and rinsed

1 large pear-shaped (Roma-type) tomato, diced

1/4 cup thinly sliced green onions

1 Bring 8 cups water to a boil in a 4- to 5-quart pan over medium-high heat. Stir in pasta and cook just until tender to bite (8 to 10 minutes); or cook according to package directions. Drain, rinse with cold water until cool, and drain well.

2 Combine vinegar, parsley, olive oil, water, honey, and chili oil in a large nonmetal bowl. Mix well. Add kidney and black beans, pasta, and tomato. Mix thoroughly but gently. Cover and refrigerate until cool (at least 30 minutes) or for up to 4 hours; stir occasionally.

3 Stir onions into pasta mixture just before serving. Transfer to a large serving bowl.

makes 4 to 6 servings

per serving: 256 calories, 11 g protein, 44 g carbohydrates, 4 g total fat, 0 mg cholesterol, 724 mg sodium

couscous tabbouleh

preparation time: about 25 minutes
chilling time: at least 30 minutes

10 ounces (about 1 2/3 cups) dried couscous

1 1/2 cups firmly packed fresh mint, minced

2 tablespoons olive oil

1/2 cup lemon juice (or to taste)

Salt and pepper

6 to 8 large butter lettuce leaves, rinsed and crisped

2 large tomatoes, thinly sliced

Mint sprigs

1 Bring 2 1/4 cups water to a boil in a 3- to 4-quart pan over high heat. Stir in pasta; cover, remove from heat, and let stand until liquid is absorbed (about 5 minutes). Transfer pasta to a large nonmetal bowl and let cool, fluffing occasionally with a fork.

2 Add minced mint, oil, and lemon juice to pasta. Season to taste with salt and pepper. Mix well. Cover and refrigerate until cool (at least 30 minutes) or for up to 4 hours; fluff occasionally with a fork.

3 Line a platter with lettuce leaves. Mound tabbouleh in center; arrange tomatoes around edge. Garnish with mint sprigs.

makes 6 to 8 servings

per serving: 210 calories, 6 g protein, 36 g carbohydrates, 5 g total fat, 0 mg cholesterol, 14 mg sodium

lentil & pappardelle salad

preparation time: about 1 hour
chilling time: at least 30 minutes

2 cups beef broth

6 ounces (about 1 cup) lentils, rinsed and drained

1 teaspoon dried oregano

6 ounces dried pappardelle or extra-wide egg noodles

1/3 cup lemon juice

3 tablespoons chopped fresh mint or 1 teaspoon dried mint

2 tablespoons olive oil

1 teaspoon honey (or to taste)

6 cups shredded red leaf lettuce leaves

1 or 2 cloves garlic, minced or pressed

2/3 cup crumbled feta cheese (or to taste)

Mint sprigs

1 Bring broth to a boil in a 1 ½- to 2-quart pan over high heat. Add lentils and oregano; reduce heat, cover, and simmer just until lentils are tender to bite (20 to 30 minutes). Drain, if necessary. Transfer to a large nonmetal bowl and let cool. Meanwhile, bring 8 cups water to a boil in a 4- to 5-quart pan over medium-high heat. Stir in pasta and cook just until tender to bite (8 to 10 minutes); or cook according to package directions. Drain, rinse with cold water until cool, and drain well.

2 Add pasta, lemon juice, chopped mint, oil, and honey to lentils. Mix thoroughly but gently. Cover and refrigerate until cool (at least 30 minutes) or for up to 4 hours; stir occasionally.

3 Arrange lettuce on a platter. Stir garlic into pasta mixture and spoon onto lettuce. Sprinkle with cheese. Garnish with mint sprigs.

makes 6 to 8 servings

per serving: 273 calories, 14 g protein, 37 g carbohydrates, 8 g total fat, 34 mg cholesterol, 619 mg sodium

melon, basil & bacon salad

preparation time: 25 minutes
cooling time: about 20 minutes

6 ounces sliced bacon

1 ½ tablespoons firmly packed brown sugar

8 cups peeled, seeded melon wedges; use any soft, aromatic melon, such as honeydew, cantaloupe, and/or crenshaw

1/4 cup lime juice

1/3 cup finely slivered fresh basil

Basil sprigs

1 Line a shallow 10- by 15-inch baking pan with foil. Arrange bacon in pan in a single layer; bake in a 350° oven for 10 minutes. Spoon off and discard drippings. Evenly pat sugar onto bacon; bake until bacon is deep golden (about 10 more minutes).

2 Lift bacon to a board; let cool slightly, then cut diagonally into ½-inch slices. In a large, shallow bowl, combine melon, lime juice, and slivered basil. Top with bacon; garnish with basil sprigs.

makes 4 servings

per serving: 210 calories, 6 g protein, 36 g carbohydrates, 7 g total fat, 10 mg cholesterol, 226 mg sodium

macaroni salad

preparation time: about 45 minutes
chilling time: at least 30 minutes

Tofu Mayonnaise (recipe follows)

8 ounces (about 2 cups) dried elbow macaroni

1 large hard-cooked egg, chopped

1/2 cup thinly sliced celery

1 jar (about 2 oz.) chopped pimentos, drained

1/2 cup chopped dill pickles

1/4 cup thinly sliced green onions

Green leaf lettuce leaves, washed and crisped

Tomato slices

Thyme or parsley sprigs

1 Prepare Tofu Mayonnaise; cover and refrigerate.

2 Bring 8 cups water to a boil in a 4- to 5-quart pan over medium-high heat. Stir in pasta and cook just until tender to bite (8 to 10 minutes); or cook according to package directions. Drain, rinse with cold water until cool, and drain well.

3 Transfer pasta to a large nonmetal bowl. Add Tofu Mayonnaise, egg, celery, pimentos, and pickles. Mix well. Cover and refrigerate until cool (at least 30 minutes) or for up to 2 hours; stir occasionally. Just before serving, stir in onions. Arrange lettuce and tomatoes on individual plates. Top with pasta. Garnish with thyme sprigs.

Makes 8 servings

TOFU MAYONNAISE

Rinse 8 ounces soft tofu in a colander. Coarsely mash tofu; let drain for 10 minutes. Transfer to a blender or food processor. Add 1/4 cup low-sodium chicken or vegetable broth, 3 tablespoons lemon juice, 2 tablespoons olive oil or salad oil, 2 teaspoons each prepared horseradish and sugar, and 1 teaspoon each dried thyme and Dijon mustard. Whirl until smooth. Season to taste with salt. If made ahead, cover and refrigerate for up to an hour. Stir before using.

per serving: 173 calories, 6 g protein, 25 g carbohydrates, 5 g total fat, 27 mg cholesterol, 165 mg sodium

ginger pear & hazelnut salad

preparation time: about 30 minutes

1/3 cup hazelnuts

1/2 cup balsamic or red wine vinegar

3 tablespoons *each* honey and minced crystallized ginger

8 small or 4 large firm-ripe Bartlett pears

2 tablespoons lemon juice

Leaf lettuce leaves, rinsed and crisped

1 Spread hazelnuts in a shallow baking pan and toast in a 350° oven until pale golden beneath skins (about 10 minutes). Let cool slightly; then rub off as much of skins as possible with your fingers. Chop nuts coarsely and set aside.

2 In a small bowl, stir together vinegar, honey, and ginger; set aside. Halve and core pears; brush cut sides with lemon juice. Line a platter with lettuce leaves; arrange pear halves, cut side up, on lettuce. Spoon dressing over pears, then sprinkle with hazelnuts.

makes 8 servings

per serving: 138 calories, 1 g protein, 29 g carbohydrates, 3 g total fat, 0 mg cholesterol, 4 mg sodium

bulgur tabbouleh salad

preparation time: 15 minutes, plus about 1 hour for bulgur to stand
chilling time: at least 30 minutes

2 cups bulgur

1 ½ cups firmly packed fresh mint leaves

1 can (about 15 oz.) garbanzo beans, drained and rinsed

About ½ cup lemon juice (or to taste)

2 tablespoons olive oil

Salt and pepper

About 8 large butter lettuce leaves, rinsed and crisped

2 large firm-ripe tomatoes, thinly sliced

4 ounces feta cheese, crumbled

Mint sprigs and lemon slices

1 In a deep bowl, mix bulgur and 2 cups cold water. Let stand until grain is tender to bite and water has been absorbed (about 1 hour), stirring occasionally.

2 Finely chop mint leaves and add to bulgur along with beans, lemon juice, and oil. Mix well; season to taste with salt and pepper. Cover and refrigerate until cool (at least 30 minutes) or for up to 4 hours.

3 Line a platter with lettuce leaves. Arrange tomatoes around edge of platter; mound tabbouleh in center and sprinkle with cheese. Garnish with mint sprigs and lemon slices.

makes 4 servings

per serving: 486 calories, 18 g protein, 74 g carbohydrates, 16 g total fat, 25 mg cholesterol, 463 mg sodium

peking spinach salad

preparation time: about 35 minutes

12 wonton skins (*each* about 3 inches square)

⅓ cup plum jam

1 tablespoon reduced-sodium soy sauce

3 tablespoons lemon juice

½ teaspoon ground cinnamon

6 cups lightly packed stemmed spinach leaves, rinsed and crisped

4 ounces mushrooms, thinly sliced

¾ cup *each* shredded carrots and lightly packed cilantro sprigs

2 medium-size red-skinned plums, pitted and thinly sliced

1 Cut each wonton skin into quarters. Arrange in a single layer on a greased baking sheet; spray or brush with water. Bake in a 500° oven until golden (about 3 minutes), watching carefully to prevent burning. Set aside.

2 In a small bowl, stir together jam, soy sauce, lemon juice, and cinnamon. Set aside.

3 Place spinach in a large bowl. Top with mushrooms, carrots, cilantro, and plums. Just before serving, add won ton skins and dressing; mix gently and serve immediately.

makes 8 servings

per serving: 99 calories, 3 g protein, 22 g carbohydrates, 0.6 g total fat, 1 mg cholesterol, 196 mg sodium

warm wild rice & asparagus salad

preparation time: 15 minutes
cooking time: about 1 hour and 20 minutes

1 cup wild rice, rinsed and drained

1 cup lentils

1 pound mushrooms, thinly sliced

1 large onion, chopped

About 2 ½ cups vegetable broth

1 pound slender asparagus

3 tablespoons balsamic vinegar

1 tablespoon olive oil

½ cup grated Parmesan cheese

1 In a 5- to 6-quart pan, combine rice and 8 cups water. Bring to a boil over high heat; then reduce heat, cover, and simmer for 30 minutes. Meanwhile, sort through lentils, discarding any debris; rinse lentils, drain, and set aside.

2 Add lentils to rice and continue to simmer until both rice and lentils are tender to bite (about 25 more minutes). Drain and let cool.

3 In a wide nonstick frying pan, combine mushrooms, onion, and ¾ cup of the broth. Cook over medium-high heat, stirring often, until liquid evaporates and browned bits stick to pan bottom (about 10 minutes). To deglaze pan, add ⅓ cup of the broth, stirring to loosen browned bits from pan; continue to cook until browned bits form again. Repeat deglazing step about 3 more times or until vegetables are browned, using ⅓ cup more broth each time.

4 Snap off and discard tough ends of asparagus; thinly slice stalks. Add asparagus and ⅓ cup more broth to mushroom mixture; cook, stirring often, until asparagus is tender-crisp to bite (about 2 minutes).

5 Spoon rice-lentil mixture into a large bowl. Add asparagus mixture, vinegar, and oil; mix gently but thoroughly. Sprinkle with cheese.

makes 8 servings

per serving: 236 calories, 15 g protein, 27 g carbohydrates, 4 g total fat, 4 mg cholesterol, 413 mg sodium

salad of leaves & fruit

preparation time: about 15 minutes

Citrus Dressing (recipe follows)

1 large orange

1 medium-size head butter lettuce, separated into leaves, rinsed, and crisped

1 head radicchio or Belgian endive, separated into leaves, rinsed, and crisped

1 cup raspberries or seedless red grapes

1 Prepare Citrus Dressing; set aside. Cut peel and all white membrane from orange. Cut between membranes to release orange segments; set aside.

2 Tear lettuce and radicchio leaves into bite-size pieces. Place leaves in a bowl and toss to mix. Then mound leaves equally on 4 individual plates; top with oranges and raspberries. Spoon Citrus Dressing over salads.

makes 4 servings

CITRUS DRESSING

In a small bowl, stir together ¼ cup orange juice, 2 tablespoons raspberry vinegar or red wine vinegar, and ½ teaspoon honey. Season to taste with salt.

per serving: 61 calories, 2 g protein, 14 g carbohydrates, 0.5 g total fat, 0 mg cholesterol, 5 mg sodium

chicken & citrus pasta salad

preparation time: about 1 1/2 hours
chilling time: at least 30 minutes

2 large oranges

Citrus Pasta Salad (recipe follows)

Orange Cream (recipe follows)

1/4 cup orange marmalade

1 teaspoon prepared horseradish

6 skinless, boneless chicken breast halves
(about 1 1/2 lbs. *total*)

2 large blood oranges or 1 small pink grapefruit

2 medium-size avocados, optional

2 tablespoons lemon juice (optional)

Basil sprigs

Finely shredded orange peel

1 Grate 4 teaspoons peel from oranges. Prepare Citrus Pasta Salad and Orange Cream, using grated peel; cover and refrigerate.

2 Mix marmalade and horseradish in a large bowl. Add chicken and stir to coat. Place chicken in a lightly oiled 10- by 15-inch baking pan. Bake in a 450° oven until meat in thickest part is no longer pink; cut to test (12 to 15 minutes). Let cool. Meanwhile, cut peel and white membrane from oranges and blood oranges; slice fruit crosswise into rounds 1/4 inch thick. (For grapefruit, cut segments from membrane; discard membrane.)

3 Arrange pasta salad and chicken on a platter. Place fruit around edge. If desired, pit, peel, and slice avocados; coat with lemon juice and place on platter. Garnish with basil sprigs and shredded orange peel. Offer Orange Cream to add to taste.

makes 6 servings

CHICKEN & CITRUS PASTA SALAD

1 Bring 12 cups water to a boil in a 5- to 6-quart pan over medium-high heat. Stir in 12 ounces (about 5 cups) dried rotini or other corkscrew-shaped pasta. Cook just until tender to bite (8 to 10 minutes); or cook according to package directions. Drain, rinse with cold water until cool, and drain well. In a large nonmetal bowl, combine 1 tablespoon grated orange peel; 3/4 cup orange juice; 1 small orange, peeled and coarsely chopped; 3 tablespoons white wine vinegar or distilled white vinegar; 3 tablespoons chopped fresh basil; 1 tablespoon each honey and Dijon mustard; 1 1/2 teaspoons ground cumin; and 1 fresh jalapeño chile, seeded and finely chopped. Mix until blended. Add pasta and mix thoroughly but gently. Cover and refrigerate until cool (at least 30 minutes) or for up to 4 hours; stir occasionally. Just before serving, stir in 1/4 cup chopped parsley and 2 or 3 cloves garlic, minced or pressed.

per serving: 463 calories, 38 g protein, 70 g carbohydrates, 4 g total fat, 74 mg cholesterol, 158 mg sodium

ORANGE CREAM

In a small nonmetal bowl, combine 1 cup nonfat or reduced-fat sour cream, 3 tablespoons orange marmalade, 2 teaspoons prepared horseradish, and 1 teaspoon grated orange peel. Mix until blended. Season to taste with ground white pepper. If made ahead, cover and refrigerate for up to a day. Stir before serving.

makes about 1 1/4 cups

per serving: 16 calories, 1 g protein, 3 g carbohydrates, 0 g total fat, 0 mg cholesterol, 10 mg sodium

quinoa & spinach salad

preparation time: about 50 minutes

½ cup quinoa

1 cinnamon stick (about 3 inches long)

½ teaspoon cumin seeds

½ cup *each* unsweetened apple juice and water

3 tablespoons dried currants

2 cans (about 15 oz. *each*) cannellini (white kidney beans), drained and rinsed

8 cups bite-size pieces rinsed, crisped fresh spinach

1 large red-skinned apple, cored and thinly sliced

⅓ cup cider vinegar

3 tablespoons honey

2 tablespoons salad oil

1 Place quinoa in a fine strainer and rinse thoroughly with cool water; drain well. Then place quinoa in a 1 ½- to 2-quart pan and cook over medium heat, stirring often, until darker in color (about 8 minutes). Add cinnamon stick, cumin seeds, apple juice, and water. Increase heat to medium-high and bring mixture to a boil; then reduce heat, cover, and simmer until almost all liquid has been absorbed and quinoa is tender to bite (about 15 minutes). Discard cinnamon stick; stir in currants and half the beans. Use quinoa mixture warm or cool.

2 In a large serving bowl, combine spinach, remaining beans, and apple. Mound quinoa mixture atop spinach mixture. In a small bowl, beat vinegar, honey, and oil until blended; pour over salad and mix gently but thoroughly.

makes 4 servings

per serving: 422 calories, 16 g protein, 72 g carbohydrates, 10 g total fat, 0 mg cholesterol, 336 mg sodium

ceviche with radishes & peas

preparation time: about 40 minutes
cooking time: at least 1½ hours

¾ cup each unseasoned rice vinegar and water; or 1 cup distilled white vinegar plus ½ cup water

2 tablespoons minced crystallized ginger

½ teaspoon coriander seeds

1 pound skinless, boneless lean, firm-textured fish such as halibut, mahi-mahi, or swordfish, cut into ½-inch chunks

1 cup frozen tiny peas, thawed

1 cup sliced red radishes

Salt and pepper

1 In a wide nonstick frying pan, bring vinegar, water, ginger, and coriander seeds to a boil over high heat. Add fish. Reduce heat, cover, and simmer until fish is just opaque but still moist in thickest part; cut to test (3 to 4 minutes). With a slotted spoon, transfer fish to a bowl.

2 Boil cooking liquid over high heat, uncovered, until reduced to 1 cup; pour over fish. Cover and refrigerate until cool (at least 1 ½ hours) or for up to 8 hours.

3 Gently mix peas and radish slices with fish. Spoon into 4 or 6 shallow soup bowls; distribute liquid equally among bowls. Season to taste with salt and pepper.

makes 4 main-dish or 6 first-course servings

per serving: 196 calories, 26 g protein, 16 g carbohydrates, 3 g total fat, 36 mg cholesterol, 137 mg sodium

wheat berry satay salad

preparation time: 15 minutes, plus about 30 minutes for salad to cool

cooking time: about 1 ³/₄ hours

2 large yellow or white onions, thinly sliced

2 cups wheat berries, rinsed and drained

3 cups vegetable broth

About ¹/₈ teaspoon crushed red pepper flakes (or to taste)

1 tablespoon finely chopped fresh ginger

2 tablespoons creamy peanut butter

2 tablespoons fruit or berry jam or jelly

2 tablespoons seasoned rice vinegar or 2 tablespoons distilled white vinegar plus ¹/₂ to 1 teaspoon sugar

About 1 tablespoon reduced-sodium soy sauce (or to taste)

1 cup chopped cilantro

1 cup sliced green onions

¹/₄ cup finely chopped salted roasted peanuts

1 In a 4- to 5-quart pan, combine yellow onions and ¹/₂ cup water. Cook over medium-high heat, stirring often, until liquid evaporates and browned bits stick to pan bottom (10 to 15 minutes). To deglaze pan, add ¹/₄ cup more water, stirring to loosen browned bits from pan; continue to cook until browned bits form again. Repeat deglazing step 3 or 4 more times or until onions are dark brown, using ¹/₄ cup water each time.

2 Add wheat berries, broth, red pepper flakes, and ginger to pan. Bring to a boil; then reduce heat, cover, and simmer, stirring occasionally, until wheat berries are just tender to bite (50 to 60 minutes). Remove from heat; drain and reserve cooking liquid.

3 In a small bowl, beat ¹/₄ cup of the reserved cooking liquid, peanut butter, and jam until smoothly blended. Stir peanut butter mixture, vinegar, and soy sauce into wheat berry mixture. Cover salad and let stand until cool (about 30 minutes).

4 Add two-thirds each of the cilantro and green onions to salad; mix gently but thoroughly. If a moister texture is desired, mix in some of the remaining cooking liquid. Transfer salad to a serving bowl; sprinkle with remaining cilantro, remaining green onions, and peanuts.

makes 4 servings

per serving: 517 calories, 19 g protein, 92 g carbohydrates, 12 g total fat, 0 mg cholesterol, 1,136 mg sodium

pineapple, strawberry & apple salad

preparation time: about 25 minutes

1 medium-size pineapple

1 small tart green-skinned apple

1 cup coarsely chopped strawberries

¹/₃ cup plain low-fat yogurt

8 to 16 butter lettuce leaves, rinsed and crisped

8 whole strawberries

1 cup small-curd cottage cheese

1 Cut peel and eyes from pineapple. Slice off top third of pineapple; cut out and discard core, then chop fruit. Place chopped pineapple in a medium-size bowl and set aside. Cut remaining pineapple lengthwise into 8 wedges; cut off and discard core from each wedge. Core apple and cut into ¹/₂-inch chunks. Add apple, chopped strawberries, and yogurt to chopped pineapple; mix lightly.

2 On each of 8 individual plates, arrange 1 or 2 lettuce leaves, a pineapple wedge, a whole strawberry, an eighth of the cottage cheese, and an eighth of the fruit mixture.

makes 8 servings

per serving: 92 calories, 4 g protein, 16 g carbohydrates, 2 g total fat, 4 mg cholesterol, 115 mg sodium

smoked salmon pasta salad

preparation time: about 30 minutes

8 ounces (about 3 cups) dried radiatorre or rotini

¼ cup seasoned rice vinegar; or ¼ cup distilled white vinegar and 2 teaspoons sugar

1 tablespoon chopped fresh dill or ½ teaspoon dried dill weed

1 tablespoon olive oil

8 cups bite-size pieces green leaf lettuce leaves

¼ cup thinly sliced red onion

2 to 4 ounces sliced smoked salmon or lox, cut into bite-size pieces

Dill sprigs

Freshly grated Parmesan cheese

1 Bring 8 cups water to a boil in a 4- to 5-quart pan over medium-high heat. Stir in pasta and cook just until tender to bite (8 to 10 minutes); or cook according to package directions. Drain, rinse with cold water until cool, and drain well.

2 Combine vinegar, chopped dill, and oil in a large nonmetal serving bowl. Mix until blended. Add pasta, lettuce, and onion. Mix thoroughly but gently. Stir in salmon. Garnish with dill sprigs. Offer cheese to add to taste.

makes 6 servings

per serving: 194 calories, 8 g protein, 32 g carbohydrates, 4 g total fat, 3 mg cholesterol, 316 mg sodium

cherry salad with orange dressing

preparation time: about 30 minutes

Orange Dressing (recipe follows)

1 medium-size head iceberg lettuce

1 small pineapple, peeled, cored, and cut into 1-inch chunks

2 ½ cups dark sweet cherries, stemmed and pitted

1 Prepare Orange Dressing; set aside.

2 Remove 4 of the largest lettuce leaves; set aside. Break remaining lettuce into bite-size pieces and place in a large bowl. Add pineapple and cherries. Pour dressing over salad and mix to coat evenly.

3 Line a salad bowl with reserved lettuce leaves; spoon in salad.

makes 6 servings

ORANGE DRESSING

Toast 2 tablespoons sesame seeds in a wide frying pan over medium-high heat until golden (2 to 4 minutes), stirring often. Pour out of pan and set aside. In a bowl, stir together 1 cup plain nonfat yogurt, 3 tablespoons each frozen orange juice concentrate (thawed) and lime juice, and ¼ teaspoon salt. Add sesame seeds; stir until well blended.

per serving: 162 calories, 5 g protein, 33 g carbohydrates, 3 g total fat, 0.8 mg cholesterol, 130 mg sodium

sweet & sour ravioli salad

preparation time: about 40 minutes
chilling time: at least 30 minutes

1 package (about 9 oz.) fresh low-fat or regular cheese ravioli or tortellini

2 pounds pear-shaped (Roma-type) tomatoes (about 10 large)

$1/2$ cup seasoned rice vinegar; or $1/2$ cup distilled white vinegar and 4 teaspoons sugar

2 tablespoons firmly packed brown sugar

$1/2$ teaspoon *each* coriander seeds, cumin seeds, and mustard seeds

$1/16$ teaspoon ground red pepper (cayenne)

Parsley sprigs

1 Bring 12 cups water to a boil in a 5- to 6-quart pan over medium-high heat. Separating any ravioli that are stuck together, add pasta. Reduce heat to medium and boil gently, stirring occasionally, just until pasta is tender to bite (4 to 6 minutes); or cook according to package directions. Lift out pasta, rinse with cold water until cool, and drain well. Transfer to a large nonmetal serving bowl and set aside.

2 Bring water in pan back to a boil. Drop in tomatoes and cook for 1 minute. Drain and let cool. Peel and discard skin; cut into bite-size pieces. Set aside.

3 Combine vinegar, brown sugar, coriander seeds, cumin seeds, mustard seeds, and ground red pepper in a 1- to 1 $1/2$-quart pan. Bring to a simmer over low heat. Cook, stirring, just until sugar is dissolved (about 1 minute).

4 Add tomatoes and vinegar mixture to pasta. Mix thoroughly but gently. Let cool briefly; then cover and refrigerate until cool (at least 30 minutes) or for up to 4 hours; stir occasionally.

5 Garnish with parsley.

makes 6 to 8 servings

per serving: 153 calories, 6 g protein, 27 g carbohydrates, 3 g total fat, 22 mg cholesterol, 481 mg sodium

strawberry tarragon dressing

preparation time: about 20 minutes

1 $1/2$ cups strawberries, hulled

About $1/4$ cup lemon juice

1 tablespoon sugar

1 tablespoon finely chopped shallot

1 teaspoon chopped fresh tarragon or $1/2$ teaspoon dried tarragon

$1/2$ teaspoon cornstarch

2 tablespoons orange juice

1 Whirl strawberries in a blender or food processor until puréed. Rub through a fine wire strainer into a 2-cup glass measure. Add $1/4$ cup of the lemon juice and enough water to make 1 cup. Transfer to a small pan and add sugar, shallot, and tarragon.

2 Smoothly mix cornstarch and orange juice; stir into strawberry mixture. Bring to a boil over high heat, stirring constantly. Set pan in a bowl of ice water to chill mixture quickly; then taste and add more lemon juice, if needed. (At this point, you may cover and refrigerate for up to a day.)

makes about 1 cup

per tablespoon: 10 calories, 0.1 g protein, 2 g carbohydrates, 0.1 g total fat, 0 mg cholesterol, 1 mg sodium

indonesian brown rice salad

preparation time: about 1 1/2 hours

BROWN RICE SALAD:

2 cups long-grain brown rice

2 cups Chinese pea pods

1 medium-size red bell pepper

5 green onions

1 can (about 8 oz.) water chestnuts, drained

1/4 cup cilantro leaves

1 cup raisins

1 cup roasted peanuts

CILANTRO SAUCE:

2 cups plain nonfat yogurt

1/2 cup cilantro leaves

1 teaspoon Asian sesame oil

1/2 teaspoon finely chopped garlic

1/4 teaspoon salt (or to taste)

LIME DRESSING:

2/3 cup unseasoned rice vinegar or cider vinegar

2 tablespoons *each* lime juice and reduced-sodium soy sauce

1 tablespoon minced fresh ginger

2 teaspoons finely chopped garlic

1 teaspoon honey

1 In a 2 1/2- to 3-quart pan, bring 4 1/2 cups water to a boil over medium-high heat. Stir in rice; then reduce heat, cover, and simmer until liquid has been absorbed and rice is tender to bite (about 45 minutes). Transfer to a large bowl and let cool, stirring occasionally.

2 Meanwhile, remove and discard ends and strings of pea pods; thinly slice pea pods. Seed and chop bell pepper. Thinly slice onions; chop water chestnuts.

3 To cooled rice, add pea pods, bell pepper, onions, water chestnuts, the 1/4 cup cilantro, raisins, and peanuts. Mix gently but thoroughly; set aside.

4 In a small serving bowl, combine yogurt, the 1/2 cup cilantro, oil, the 1/2 teaspoon garlic, and salt. Stir until blended; set aside.

5 In another small bowl, combine vinegar, lime juice, soy sauce, ginger, the 2 teaspoons garlic, and honey. Beat until blended; pour over salad and mix gently but thoroughly. Serve salad with cilantro sauce.

makes 8 servings

per serving: 545 calories, 18 g protein, 90 g carbohydrates, 15 g total fat, 2 mg cholesterol, 560 mg sodium

PLAN-AHEAD SALADS: Advance planning can provide you with leftover meat and poultry for main-dish salads. If you're roasting one chicken for Sunday dinner, roast a second one alongside—and use the extra meat in a salad later in the week. Keep in mind that a 3-pound frying chicken will yield about 3 cups meat; a 1-pound whole chicken breast will yield about 1 1/2 cups meat. A half pound of cooked boneless ham, beef, or turkey will yield about 2 cups meat. Keep hard-cooked eggs in the refrigerator (marked to distinguish them from raw eggs). A common ingredient in main-dish salads, they also add extra flavor and a protein boost to side-dish salads. Slice or chop the eggs coarsely and toss them with the salad; or cut into wedges and use as a garnish.

steak, couscous & greens with raspberries

preparation time: about 1 1/4 hours
marinating time: at least 30 minutes
chilling time: at least 30 minutes

1 pound lean boneless top sirloin steak (about
    1 inch thick), trimmed of fat

1/2 cup dry red wine

5 tablespoons raspberry vinegar or red wine
    vinegar

1/4 cup chopped green onions

2 tablespoons reduced-sodium soy sauce

1 tablespoon sugar

2 teaspoons chopped fresh tarragon or
    1/2 teaspoon dried tarragon

1 tablespoon raspberry or apple jelly

3/4 cup low-sodium chicken broth

2/3 cup low-fat milk

1/4 teaspoon ground coriander

6 1/2 ounces (about 1 cup) dried couscous

1 tablespoon olive oil

8 cups bite-size pieces red leaf lettuce leaves

2 cups raspberries

Tarragon sprigs (optional)

1 Slice steak across grain into strips about 1/8 inch thick and 3 inches long. Place meat, wine, 1 tablespoon of the vinegar, 2 tablespoons of the onions, soy sauce, 2 teaspoons of the sugar, and chopped tarragon in a large heavy-duty resealable plastic bag or large nonmetal bowl. Seal bag and rotate to coat meat (or stir meat in bowl and cover airtight). Refrigerate for at least 30 minutes or up to a day, turning (or stirring) occasionally.

2 Cook jelly in a 2- to 3-quart pan over low heat, stirring, until melted. Add broth, milk, and coriander; increase heat to medium-high and bring to a gentle boil. Stir in couscous. Cover, remove from heat, and let stand until liquid is absorbed (about 5 minutes).

3 Transfer couscous mixture to a large nonmetal bowl; let cool briefly, fluffing occasionally with a fork. Cover and refrigerate until cool (at least 30 minutes) or for up to 2 hours, fluffing occasionally. Meanwhile, heat 1 teaspoon of the oil in a wide nonstick frying pan over medium-high heat. Add meat and its juices and cook, stirring, until browned and done to your liking; cut to test (3 to 5 minutes). Transfer to a large nonmetal bowl and let cool.

4 Combine remaining 2 teaspoons oil, remaining 4 tablespoons vinegar, and remaining 1 teaspoon sugar in a large nonmetal bowl. Mix until blended. Add lettuce and turn to coat. Arrange lettuce on individual plates. Stir remaining 2 tablespoons onions into couscous mixture. Spoon onto lettuce, top with meat, and sprinkle with raspberries. Garnish with tarragon sprigs, if desired.

makes 4 servings

per serving: 456 calories, 34 g protein, 55 g carbohydrates, 10 g total fat, 71 mg cholesterol, 273 mg sodium

creamy herb dressing

1 cup plain nonfat yogurt

3 tablespoons balsamic vinegar

1 1/2 teaspoons chopped fresh oregano or
    1/4 teaspoon dried oregano

1 teaspoon Dijon mustard

2 to 3 teaspoons sugar

In a nonmetal bowl, mix yogurt, vinegar, oregano, mustard, and sugar. If made ahead, cover and refrigerate for up to 3 days.

makes 1 1/4 cups

per tablespoon: 9 calories, 0.6 g protein, 1 g carbohydrates, 0 g total fat, 0.2 mg cholesterol, 15 mg sodium

curried shrimp & shell salad

preparation time: about 25 minutes
cooking time: about 15 minutes
chilling time: at least 30 minutes

Curry Dressing (recipe follows)

2 ounces (about ¹/₂ cup) dried small shell-shaped pasta

12 ounces tiny cooked shrimp

1 cup coarsely chopped cucumber

3 tablespoons dried tomatoes packed in oil, drained well and coarsely chopped

Salt

4 to 8 large butter lettuce leaves, rinsed and crisped

Lemon wedges

1 Prepare Curry Dressing; cover and refrigerate.

2 Bring 4 cups water to a boil in a 3- to 4-quart pan over medium-high heat. Stir in pasta and cook just until tender to bite (8 to 10 minutes); or cook according to package directions. Drain, rinse with cold water until cool, and drain well. Transfer pasta to a large nonmetal bowl. Add shrimp, cucumber, tomatoes, and dressing. Mix thoroughly but gently. Season to taste with salt. Cover and refrigerate until cool (at least 30 minutes) or for up to 4 hours; stir occasionally.

3 Arrange lettuce on individual plates. Spoon pasta mixture onto lettuce. Offer lemon to add to taste.

CURRY DRESSING

In a small nonmetal bowl, combine ¹/₄ cup nonfat or reduced-calorie mayonnaise, 1 tablespoon Dijon mustard, ¹/₂ teaspoon grated lemon peel, 1 tablespoon lemon juice, 1 teaspoon each dried dill weed and honey, ¹/₂ teaspoon curry powder, and ¹/₄ teaspoon pepper. Mix until blended. If made ahead, cover and refrigerate for up to an hour. Stir before using.

makes 4 servings

per serving: 226 calories, 21 g protein, 19 g carbohydrates, 7 g total fat, 166 mg cholesterol, 395 mg sodium

green & white sesame salad

preparation time: about 25 minutes

¹/₃ cup seasoned rice vinegar (or ¹/₃ cup distilled white vinegar plus 1 tablespoon sugar)

1 tablespoon *each* sugar, hoisin sauce, and Dijon mustard

3 tablespoons sesame seeds

1 pound slender asparagus, tough ends removed

10 to 12 ounces slender green beans, ends removed

12 ounces jicama, peeled and cut into long matchstick strips

1 In a small bowl, stir together vinegar, sugar, hoisin sauce, and mustard. Set aside.

2 Toast sesame seeds in a wide frying pan over medium-high heat until golden (2 to 4 minutes), stirring often. Add to dressing and stir to mix.

3 Pour water into frying pan to a depth of ¹/₂-inch and bring to a boil over high heat. Add asparagus and beans. Cover and cook just until vegetables are tender-crisp to bite (2 to 3 minutes). Drain, immerse in cold water until cool, and drain again.

4 Arrange asparagus, beans, and jicama on a platter. Stir dressing well; drizzle over vegetables.

makes 6 servings

per serving: 100 calories, 4 g protein, 17 g carbohydrates, 3 g total fat, 0 mg cholesterol, 429 mg sodium

shrimp & orzo with pesto dressing

preparation time: about 35 minutes

Pesto Dressing (recipe follows)

6 cups low-sodium chicken broth

8 ounces (about 1 1/3 cups) dried orzo or other rice-shaped pasta

1 pound tiny cooked shrimp

1 cup chopped green onions

1 tablespoon grated lemon peel

1/2 cup lemon juice

1 small head iceberg lettuce, rinsed and crisped

3 cups tiny cherry tomatoes

1 Prepare Pesto Dressing; cover and refrigerate.

2 Bring broth to a boil in a 4- to 5-quart pan over medium-high heat. Stir in pasta and cook just until barely tender to bite (about 5 minutes). Drain well, reserving liquid for other uses. Let cool completely.

3 Transfer pasta to a large bowl. Add shrimp, onions, lemon peel, and lemon juice. Mix thoroughly but gently.

4 Shred lettuce and place in a shallow serving bowl. Spoon pasta mixture into bowl. Arrange tomatoes around edge of bowl. Offer dressing to add to taste.

makes 5 or 6 servings

per serving: 274 calories, 26 g protein, 38 g carbohydrates, 4 g total fat, 148 mg cholesterol, 305 mg sodium

PESTO DRESSING

In a blender or food processor, combine 1/2 cup each chopped fresh basil and chopped cilantro, 1 cup plain nonfat yogurt, and 1 tablespoon white wine vinegar. Whirl until smooth. If made ahead, cover and refrigerate for up to 4 hours. Stir before serving.

makes about 1 1/4 cups

per serving: 8 calories, 0.7 g protein, 1 g carbohydrates, 0 g total fat, 0.2 mg cholesterol, 9 mg sodium

carrot slaw

preparation time: about 20 minutes
chilling time: at least 1 hour

1 1/2 pounds carrots, shredded

1 teaspoon grated lime peel

1/3 cup lime juice

2 tablespoons *each* distilled white vinegar and honey

1 tablespoon Dijon mustard

1 teaspoon caraway seeds

1/4 teaspoon crushed red pepper flakes

Salt

In a medium-size bowl, combine carrots, lime peel, lime juice, vinegar, honey, mustard, caraway seeds, and red pepper flakes. Mix gently; then season to taste with salt. Cover and refrigerate until cold (at least 1 hour) or for up to 2 days. To serve, lift to individual plates with a slotted spoon.

makes 4 to 6 servings

per serving: 94 calories, 2 g protein, 23 g carbohydrates, 0.5 g total fat, 0 mg cholesterol, 141 mg sodium

spinach salad with garlic croutons

preparation time: about 25 minutes

1 1/2 pounds spinach, stems removed, leaves rinsed and crisped

1 medium-size red onion, thinly sliced and separated into rings

8 ounces mushrooms, thinly sliced

1 large red bell pepper, seeded and thinly sliced

2 ounces feta cheese, crumbled

1/2 cup lemon juice

4 teaspoons olive oil

1/2 teaspoon dry oregano

2 cloves garlic, peeled

1 small French bread baguette, cut into 1/2-inch-thick slices

1 Tear spinach leaves into bite-size pieces, if desired. Place spinach, onion, mushrooms, and bell pepper in a large bowl; set aside.

2 In a blender, whirl cheese, lemon juice, oil, oregano, and 1 clove of the garlic until smoothly blended; set aside.

3 Place baguette slices in a single layer on a baking sheet and broil about 5 inches below heat, turning once, until golden on both sides (about 4 minutes). Let toast slices cool briefly. Rub remaining garlic clove evenly over top of each toast slice; then discard garlic clove.

4 Pour dressing over salad and mix gently. Spoon salad onto individual plates. Arrange toasted baguette slices atop salads (or arrange toast on a plate and serve on the side).

makes 6 servings

per serving: 208 calories, 9 g protein, 31 g carbohydrates, 7 g total fat, 8 mg cholesterol, 410 mg sodium

chili potato salad

preparation time: about 45 minutes
cooling time: about 30 minutes

1 1/2 pounds large thin-skinned potatoes, scrubbed

1 can (about 17 oz.) corn kernels, drained

1/2 cup *each* sliced celery and chopped red onion

2/3 cup chopped red bell pepper

2 tablespoons salad oil

1/4 cup cider vinegar

2 teaspoons chili powder

1 clove garlic, minced or pressed

1/2 teaspoon liquid hot pepper seasoning

Salt and pepper

1 Place unpeeled potatoes in a 5- to 6-quart pan and add enough water to cover. Bring to a boil over high heat; then reduce heat, partially cover, and boil gently until potatoes are tender when pierced (25 to 30 minutes). Drain, immerse in cold water until cool, and drain again. Cut into 3/4-inch cubes.

2 In a large bowl, combine potatoes, corn, celery, onion, and bell pepper. Add oil, vinegar, chili powder, garlic, and hot pepper seasoning; mix gently, then season to taste with salt and pepper. If made ahead, cover and refrigerate for up to 1 day. Serve cold or at room temperature.

makes 6 servings

per serving: 210 calories, 5 g protein, 39 g carbohydrates, 5 g total fat, 0 mg cholesterol, 257 mg sodium

golden pepper salad

preparation time: about 25 minutes

Golden Dressing (recipe follows)

1 head red leaf lettuce

1 small head red oak leaf lettuce

1 small head chicory

1 large bunch watercress

1 head Belgian endive

1 _each_ medium-size yellow and red bell pepper

1 can (about 15 oz.) garbanzo beans, drained and rinsed; or 2 cups cooked garbanzo beans, drained and rinsed

1 Prepare Golden Dressing; set aside.

2 Separate lettuces into leaves (tear larger leaf lettuce leaves in half). Discard outer leaves from chicory. Discard tough stems from watercress. Rinse and crisp lettuces, chicory, and watercress; then place all greens in a 3- to 4-quart bowl.

3 Cut endive in half lengthwise, then cut each half crosswise into thin strips. Cut bell peppers in half lengthwise; remove seeds, then cut each pepper half crosswise into thin strips. Add endive, bell peppers, and beans to bowl of greens.

4 Stir Golden Dressing to blend, pour over salad, and mix gently.

makes 8 servings

GOLDEN DRESSING

In a blender or food processor, combine 1 tablespoon olive oil, ½ cup diced yellow bell pepper, 1 tablespoon minced shallot, and ⅛ teaspoon each salt and ground red pepper (cayenne). Whirl until mixture is smoothly puréed. (At this point, you may cover dressing and refrigerate for up to 1 day.) Just before using, add 2 tablespoons white wine vinegar and stir until thoroughly blended.

per serving: 84 calories, 4 g protein, 12 g carbohydrates, 3 g total fat, 0 mg cholesterol, 125 mg sodium

green pea salad

preparation time: 15 minutes
chilling time: at least 3 hours

⅓ cup plain low-fat yogurt

1 ½ tablespoons Dijon mustard

⅛ teaspoon pepper

1 package (about 10 oz.) frozen tiny peas, thawed

1 hard-cooked large egg, chopped

½ cup finely chopped red or green bell pepper

⅓ cup thinly sliced green onions

¼ cup thinly sliced celery

Butter lettuce leaves, rinsed and crisped

1 In a large bowl, stir together yogurt, mustard, and pepper. Add peas, egg, bell pepper, onions, and celery. Mix gently. Cover and refrigerate for at least 3 hours or up to 1 day.

2 To serve, line a platter or individual plates with lettuce; spoon salad onto lettuce.

makes 6 servings

per serving: 61 calories, 4 g protein, 8 g carbohydrates, 2 g total fat, 36 mg cholesterol, 201 mg sodium

beef & bow-tie salad

preparation time: about 50 minutes
marinating time: at least 30 minutes
chilling time: at least 30 minutes

1 pound lean boneless top sirloin steak (about 1 inch thick), trimmed of fat

2 tablespoons dry sherry

Blue Cheese Dressing (recipe follows)

6 to 8 ounces (3 to 4 cups) dried farfalle (about 1½-inch size)

¼ cup red wine vinegar

1 tablespoon olive oil or salad oil

1 tablespoon chopped fresh thyme or 1 teaspoon dried thyme

1 teaspoon sugar

Salt and pepper

8 cups bite-size pieces butter lettuce leaves

Thyme sprigs

1 Slice steak across grain into strips about ⅛-inch thick and 3 inches long. Place meat and sherry in a large heavy-duty resealable plastic bag or nonmetal bowl. Seal bag and rotate to coat meat (or stir meat in bowl and cover airtight). Refrigerate for at least 30 minutes or up to a day, turning (or stirring) occasionally.

2 Prepare Blue Cheese Dressing; cover and refrigerate.

3 Bring 8 cups water to a boil in a 4- to 5-quart pan over medium-high heat. Stir in pasta and cook just until tender to bite (8 to 10 minutes); or cook according to package directions. Drain, rinse with cold water until cool, and drain well.

4 Combine vinegar, 2 teaspoons of the oil, chopped thyme, and sugar in a large nonmetal bowl. Stir until blended. Add pasta and mix thoroughly but gently. Cover and refrigerate until cool (at least 30 minutes) or for up to 2 hours; stir occasionally. Meanwhile, heat remaining 1 teaspoon oil in a wide nonstick frying pan over medium-high heat. Add steak and its juices and cook, stirring, until browned and done to your liking; cut to test (3 to 5 minutes). Transfer to a large nonmetal bowl and let cool. Season to taste with salt and pepper.

5 Combine lettuce and dressing in a large serving bowl; turn to coat. Add beef to pasta mixture and stir gently. Spoon onto greens. Garnish with thyme sprigs.

makes 4 to 6 servings

BLUE CHEESE DRESSING

In a blender or food processor, combine 4 ounces low-fat (1%) or soft tofu, rinsed and drained; ¼ cup low-fat buttermilk; 1 tablespoon white wine vinegar; 2 teaspoons each sugar and olive oil; 1 teaspoon Dijon mustard; and 1 clove garlic. Whirl until smooth. Season to taste with salt and pepper. Gently stir in ¼ cup crumbled blue-veined cheese. (At this point, you may cover and refrigerate for up to an hour.) Stir in 1 tablespoon chopped green onion before using.

per serving: 376 calories, 28 g protein, 36 g carbohydrates, 12 g total fat, 61 mg cholesterol, 210 mg sodium

chicken salad with kumquats

preparation time: about 35 minutes
standing time: about 20 minutes

1 ¹/₂ **pounds chicken breast halves, skinned**

Ginger-Mint Dressing (recipe follows)

³/₄ **cup kumquats, thinly sliced, seeds and ends discarded**

1 small cucumber, cut in half lengthwise, then thinly sliced crosswise

16 Belgian endive spears or 8 large radicchio leaves, rinsed and crisped

Mint sprigs (optional)

1 In a 5- to 6-quart pan, bring about 3 quarts water to a boil over high heat. Rinse chicken and add to water; return to a boil. Then cover pan tightly, remove from heat, and let stand until meat in thickest part is no longer pink; cut to test (about 20 minutes). If chicken is not done after 20 minutes, return it to water, cover pan; and let stand longer, checking at 2- to 3-minute intervals. Remove chicken from water and let cool; then tear meat into shreds and discard bones. (At this point, you may cover and refrigerate until next day.)

2 Prepare Ginger-Mint Dressing

3 Add kumquats to bowl with dressing; mix gently. Mix in cucumber and chicken. On each of 4 individual plates, place 4 endive spears or 2 radicchio leaves; top equally with chicken mixture. Garnish with mint sprigs, if desired.

makes 4 servings

GINGER-MINT DRESSING

In a large bowl, combine ¹/₂ cup lemon juice, ¹/₄ cup finely shredded fresh mint or 2 tablespoons dry mint, 2 tablespoons each water and minced crystallized ginger, 2 ¹/₂ teaspoons sugar, and 1 tablespoon fish sauce (*nam pla* or *nuoc mam*) or reduced-sodium soy sauce.

per serving: 211 calories, 28 g protein, 21 g carbohydrates, 2 g total fat, 65 mg cholesterol, 90 mg sodium

golden potato salad

preparation time: about 50 minutes
cooling time: about 30 minutes

3 ¹/₂ **pounds small red thin-skinned potatoes, scrubbed**

8 ounces slender green beans, ends removed

³/₄ **cup chopped yellow bell pepper**

About ¹/₃ **cup low-sodium chicken broth**

3 tablespoons red wine vinegar

1 tablespoon *each* **balsamic vinegar and olive oil**

1 teaspoon *each* **ground turmeric, crushed anise seeds, and dry tarragon**

Salt and pepper

1 Place unpeeled potatoes in a 5- to 6-quart pan and add enough water to cover. Bring to a boil; reduce heat, partially cover, and boil gently until potatoes are tender when pierced (about 25 minutes). Lift out with a slotted spoon and let stand until cool (about 30 minutes). Meanwhile, return water in pan to a boil over high heat. Add beans and cook, uncovered, just until tender-crisp to bite (2 to 3 minutes). Drain, immerse in cold water until cool, and drain again. Cut potatoes into ¹/₂-inch-thick slices; cut beans into 1-inch lengths.

2 In a large bowl, combine bell pepper, ¹/₃ cup of the broth, red wine vinegar, balsamic vinegar, oil, turmeric, anise seeds, and tarragon. Add potatoes and beans; mix gently. For a moister salad, add a little more broth. Season to taste with salt and pepper.

makes 8 servings

per serving: 190 calories, 5 g protein, 39 g carbohydrates, 2 g total fat, 0 mg cholesterol, 19 mg sodium

gingered pork & ziti salad

preparation time: about 45 minutes

chilling time: at least 30 minutes

6 ounces (about 2 cups) dried ziti or penne

2/3 cup mango or pear nectar

1 tablespoon minced fresh ginger

2 teaspoons olive oil

1 or 2 cloves garlic, minced or pressed

1 teaspoon Asian sesame oil

1 1/2 cups roasted or Chinese-style barbecued pork, cut into thin 1/2-inch pieces

1/3 cup chopped red bell pepper

4 to 8 red leaf lettuce leaves, rinsed and crisped

1/4 cup thinly sliced green onions

4 whole green onions (optional)

Salt and pepper

1 Bring 8 cups water to a boil in a 4- to 5-quart pan over medium-high heat. Stir in pasta and cook just until tender to bite (8 to 10 minutes); or cook according to package directions. Drain, rinse with cold water until cool, and drain well.

2 Combine mango nectar, ginger, olive oil, garlic, and sesame oil in a large nonmetal bowl. Mix until blended. Add pasta, pork, and bell pepper. Mix thoroughly but gently. Cover and refrigerate until cool (at least 30 minutes) or for up to 3 hours; stir occasionally.

3 Arrange lettuce on individual plates. Stir sliced onions into pasta mixture and spoon onto lettuce. Garnish with whole onions, if desired. Offer salt and pepper to add to taste.

makes 4 servings

per serving: 346 calories, 24 g protein, 40 g carbohydrates, 10 g total fat, 50 mg cholesterol, 51 mg sodium

shrimp & jicama with chile vinegar

preparation time: about 35 minutes

Chile Vinegar (recipe follows)

2 cups shredded jicama

1 pound small cooked shrimp

4 large ripe tomatoes, sliced

4 large tomatillos, husked, rinsed, and sliced

Cilantro sprigs

1 Prepare Chile Vinegar. Place jicama and shrimp in separate bowls. Add 1/4 cup of the Chile Vinegar to each bowl; mix gently. Reserve remaining vinegar.

2 On each of 4 individual plates, arrange tomatoes and tomatillos, overlapping slices slightly. Mound jicama over or beside tomato slices. Spoon shrimp over jicama; spoon remaining Chile Vinegar over all. Garnish with cilantro sprigs.

CHILE VINEGAR

In a small bowl, stir together 2/3 cup white wine vinegar, 1/4 cup sugar, 2 to 3 tablespoons seeded, minced fresh hot green chiles, and 3 to 4 tablespoons chopped cilantro.

makes 4 servings

per serving: 261 calories, 28 g protein, 34 g carbohydrates, 2 g total fat, 221 mg cholesterol, 279 mg sodium

pork & rotini salad with oranges

preparation time: 1 hour
chilling time: at least 30 minutes

8 ounces (about 3 1/2 cups) dried rotini or other corkscrew-shaped pasta

1 teaspoon salad oil

1 pound pork tenderloin or boned pork loin, trimmed of fat, sliced into thin strips 1/2 inch wide

1 tablespoon minced garlic

1 teaspoon *each* chili powder and dried oregano

3/4 cup lime juice

3 tablespoons sugar

1 teaspoon reduced-sodium soy sauce

1/3 cup chopped cilantro

6 large oranges

About 40 large spinach leaves, coarse stems removed, rinsed and crisped

1 Bring 8 cups water to a boil in a 4- to 5-quart pan over medium-high heat. Stir in pasta and cook just until tender to bite (8 to 10 minutes); or cook according to package directions. Drain, rinse with cold water until cool, and drain well; set aside.

2 Heat oil in a wide nonstick frying pan over medium-high heat. Add pork, garlic, chili powder, and oregano. Cook, stirring, until pork is no longer pink in center; cut to test (about 5 minutes). Remove pan from heat and add lime juice, sugar, and soy sauce; stir to loosen browned bits. Transfer to a large nonmetal bowl and let cool briefly. Add pasta and cilantro. Mix thoroughly but gently. Cover and refrigerate until cool (at least 30 minutes) or for up to 2 hours; stir occasionally.

3 Cut peel and white membrane from oranges; thinly slice fruit crosswise. Arrange spinach on individual plates. Top with orange slices and pasta mixture.

makes 6 servings

per serving: 362 calories, 23 g protein, 59 g carbohydrates, 5 g total fat, 49 mg cholesterol, 99 mg sodium

pesto-orange potato salad

preparation time: about 25 minutes

2 medium-size oranges

1/2 cup *each* lightly packed parsley sprigs and cilantro leaves

1/4 cup grated Parmesan cheese

3/4 cup plain low-fat yogurt

1 teaspoon sugar

2 pounds russet potatoes, cooked, peeled, and cut into 1/2-inch cubes

Salt and pepper

1/2 cup walnut halves

1 Grate 2 teaspoons peel (colored part only) from oranges; set peel aside. Cut remaining peel and all white membrane from oranges. Holding fruit over a bowl to catch juice, cut between membranes to release orange segments; set segments aside.

2 Pour juice in bowl into a blender or food processor; add the 2 teaspoons grated orange peel, parsley, cilantro, cheese, yogurt, and sugar. Whirl until smooth.

3 Place potatoes in a large bowl; pour yogurt mixture over potatoes and mix gently. Season to taste with salt and pepper. Garnish with orange segments and walnuts.

makes 6 to 8 servings

per serving: 196 calories, 6 g protein, 31 g carbohydrates, 6 g total fat, 4 mg cholesterol, 82 mg sodium

chef's salad with fruit

preparation time: about 25 minutes

Honey-Mustard Dressing (recipe follows)

12 cups bite-size pieces red leaf lettuce, rinsed and crisped

2 large red Bartlett or other firm-ripe pears

4 kiwi fruit, peeled and thinly sliced crosswise

2 large carrots, coarsely grated

3 ounces part-skin mozzarella cheese, finely shredded

¼ pound thinly sliced cooked skinless turkey breast, cut into julienne strips

1 Prepare Honey-Mustard Dressing and set aside.

2 Place lettuce in a large shallow bowl or on a platter. Core and slice pears. Arrange pears, kiwis, carrots, mozzarella, and turkey in separate mounds on lettuce. Offer with dressing.

HONEY-MUSTARD DRESSING

Mix ½ cup cider vinegar, 3 tablespoons each salad oil and honey, and 2 teaspoons dry mustard. If made ahead, cover and refrigerate for up to 2 days.

makes 6 servings

per serving: 286 calories, 12 g protein, 40 g carbohydrates, 11 g total fat, 21 mg cholesterol, 110 mg sodium

caesar salad

preparation time: about 15 minutes

Garlic Croutons (recipe follows)

⅔ cup nonfat or reduced fat sour cream

1 or 2 cloves garlic, minced or pressed

2 tablespoons lemon juice

1 teaspoon Worcestershire (optional)

6 to 8 canned anchovy fillets, rinsed, drained, patted dry, and finely chopped

8 cups lightly packed bite-size pieces of rinsed, crisped romaine lettuce

About ¼ cup grated Parmesan cheese

1 Prepare Garlic Croutons; set aside.

2 In a large nonmetal bowl, beat sour cream, garlic, lemon juice, and Worcestershire (if desired) until blended. Stir in anchovies.

3 Add lettuce to bowl with dressing; mix gently but thoroughly to coat with dressing. Spoon salad onto individual plates and add cheese and croutons to taste.

makes 4 to 6 servings

GARLIC CROUTONS

In a small bowl, combine 1 tablespoon olive oil, 1 tablespoon water, and 1 clove garlic, minced or pressed. Cut 3 ounces (about 3 slices) French bread into ¾-inch cubes and spread in a 10- by 15-inch nonstick rimmed baking pan. Brush oil mixture evenly over bread cubes. Bake in a 350° oven until croutons are crisp and golden (10 to 12 minutes). If made ahead, let cool; then store airtight for up to 2 days.

makes about 3 cups

per serving: 70 calories, 7 g protein, 5 g carbohydrates, 2 g total fat, 6 mg cholesterol, 311 mg sodium

orange & olive patio salad

preparation time: about 20 minutes
cooling time: about 1 hour

¹/₂ cup water

1 teaspoon arrowroot

4 teaspoons honey

2 tablespoons finely chopped fresh mint

1 small mild red onion, thinly sliced crosswise

¹/₄ cup red wine vinegar

6 cups lightly packed mixed bite-size pieces of butter lettuce and radicchio (or all butter lettuce), rinsed and crisped

6 cups lightly packed watercress sprigs, rinsed and crisped

2 medium-size oranges, peeled and thinly sliced crosswise

¹/₄ cup small pitted ripe or Niçoise olives

¹/₄ cup lime juice

About ¹/₄ cup mixed fresh basil and fresh mint leaves (optional)

Salt and pepper

1 In a small pan, combine water, arrowroot, honey, and chopped mint. Bring to a boil over high heat, stirring constantly. Remove from heat and let stand until cold (about 1 hour).

2 Meanwhile, in a large salad bowl, combine onion and vinegar. Let stand for at least 15 minutes or up to 3 hours. Drain, discarding vinegar; separate onion slices into rings.

3 In same salad bowl, combine onion rings, lettuce, radicchio, and watercress; mix lightly. Top with orange slices and olives.

4 Stir lime juice into honey-mint mixture, then pour through a fine wire strainer over salad; discard residue. Garnish with basil and mint leaves, if desired; season to taste with salt and pepper.

makes 8 to 10 servings

per serving: 49 calories, 2 g protein, 11 g carbohydrates, 0.6 g total fat, 0 mg cholesterol, 49 mg sodium

curry oil

preparation time: About 10 minutes

¹/₄ cup curry powder

1 cup vegetable oil or olive oil

1 to 3 cinnamon sticks (*each* about 3 inches long)

1 In a small pan, whisk together curry powder and ¼ cup of the oil until well blended. Gradually whisk in remaining ¾ cup oil. Add cinnamon stick(s). Heat over medium heat, stirring often, just until warm (not hot or boiling). Remove from heat and let cool slightly.

2 With a clean, dry slotted spoon, lift out cinnamon stick(s); set aside. Carefully pour oil into a clean, dry glass bottle or jar, leaving curry sediment behind; discard sediment. (Or strain oil, if desired.) Add cinnamon stick(s) to bottle; cover airtight and store for up to 6 months.

makes about 1 cup

per tablespoon: 125 calories, 0.2 g protein, 1 g carbohydrates, 14 g total fat, 0 mg cholesterol, 0.8 mg sodium

thai coleslaw

preparation time: about 40 minutes

$^1\!/_3$ cup *each* unseasoned rice vinegar and lime juice

$^1\!/_4$ cup slivered red pickled ginger

2 small fresh serrano or jalapeño chiles, seeded and finely chopped

1 tablespoon *each* sugar and Asian sesame oil

1 tablespoon fish sauce (*nam pla* or *nuoc mam*)

$^1\!/_2$ teaspoon wasabi (green horseradish) powder

2 teaspoons sesame seeds

About 1 pound bok choy (coarse outer leaves removed), rinsed and crisped

1 small red onion, cut into thin slivers

2 medium-size carrots, thinly sliced

8 cups finely slivered Savoy or green cabbage

1 small head radicchio, cut into thin slivers

1 In a small bowl, stir together vinegar, lime juice, ginger, chiles, sugar, oil, fish sauce, and wasabi powder; set aside.

2 Toast sesame seeds in small frying pan over medium-high heat until golden (2 to 4 minutes), stirring often. Pour out of pan and set aside.

3 Thinly slice bok choy and place in a large bowl. Add onion, carrots, cabbage, radicchio, and dressing; mix gently. Sprinkle with sesame seeds.

makes 8 to 12 servings

per serving: 62 calories, 3 g protein, 10 g carbohydrates, 2 g total fat, 0 mg cholesterol, 64 mg sodium

viennese potato salad

preparation time: about 1 hour

2 $^1\!/_2$ pounds small red thin-skinned potatoes, scrubbed

$^1\!/_2$ cup pecan or walnut pieces

3 large red-skinned apples

$^1\!/_2$ cup sliced green onions cup raisins

$^1\!/_3$ cup late-harvest gewürztraminer or Johannesburg Riesling

$^1\!/_3$ cup cider vinegar

2 tablespoons salad oil

1 tablespoon grated lemon peel

2 teaspoons poppy seeds

1 Place unpeeled potatoes in a 5- to 6-quart pan and add enough water to cover. Bring to a boil over high heat; then reduce heat, partially cover, and boil gently until potatoes are tender when pierced (about 25 minutes). Drain, immerse in cold water until cool, and drain again. Cut into 1-inch cubes and set aside.

2 Toast pecans in a wide frying pan over medium-high heat until lightly browned and fragrant (about 3 minutes), stirring often. Pour out of pan and let cool; chop coarsely and set aside.

3 Core 2 of the apples and cut fruit into 1-inch chunks (set remaining apple aside to use for garnish). In a large bowl, combine apple chunks, potatoes, pecans, onions, raisins, wine, vinegar, oil, lemon peel, and poppy seeds; mix gently. If made ahead, cover and refrigerate for up to 6 hours.

4 To serve, mound salad on a large rimmed platter. Core remaining apple and cut into slices; fan slices out next to salad along one side of platter.

makes 6 to 8 servings

per serving: 307 calories, 4 g protein, 51 g carbohydrates, 10 g total fat, 0 mg cholesterol, 15 mg sodium

sweet potato & ginger salad

preparation time: about 30 minutes

¹/₂ pound sweet potatoes

2 tablespoons lemon juice

1 medium-large pineapple

1 cup finely shredded peeled jicama

2 tablespoons salad oil

2 teaspoons honey

1 teaspoon *each* minced fresh ginger and grated lemon peel

Finely chopped parsley

Red leaf lettuce leaves

1 In a 5-quart pan, bring about 3 quarts water to a boil over high heat. Peel and shred sweet potatoes; immediately add to boiling water. Cook for 30 seconds, then drain well and mix with lemon juice.

2 Cut off pineapple peel. Cut about half the pineapple into 4 crosswise slices, cover, and refrigerate. Core and finely chop remaining pineapple; drain briefly in a colander.

3 Squeeze excess liquid from jicama. Mix jicama, chopped pineapple, oil, honey, ginger, and lemon peel with sweet potatoes. (At this point, you may cover and let stand at room temperature for up to 4 hours.)

4 To serve, place an equal portion of jicama mixture atop each pineapple slice. Sprinkle with parsley and present on a lettuce-lined platter.

makes 4 servings

per serving: 244 calories, 2 g protein, 45 g carbohydrates, 8 g total fat, 0 mg cholesterol, 11 mg sodium

summer fruit & almond salad

preparation time: about 50 minutes

¹/₂ cup sliced almonds

8 ounces jicama, peeled and cut into matchstick pieces

¹/₄ cup orange juice

2 tablespoons lemon juice

1 teaspoon each poppy seeds and sugar

¹/₄ teaspoon almond extract

2 cups cubed, seeded watermelon

2 cups cubed cantaloupe

1 cup seedless grapes, halved

1 cup strawberries, hulled and sliced

12 to 16 large lettuce leaves, rinsed and crisped

1 large kiwi fruit, peeled and thinly sliced

1 Toast almonds in a wide frying pan over medium-high heat until golden (about 3 minutes), stirring often. Pour out of pan and set aside.

2 In a large bowl, mix jicama, orange juice, lemon juice, poppy seeds, sugar, and almond extract. Add watermelon, cantaloupe, grapes, and strawberries; mix gently.

3 Arrange lettuce leaves on 6 to 8 individual plates; evenly mound fruit mixture on lettuce. Garnish salad with kiwi fruit and almonds.

makes 6 to 8 servings

per serving: 128 calories, 3 g protein, 21 g carbohydrates, 4 g total fat, 0 mg cholesterol, 12 mg sodium

potato salad with seed vinaigrette

preparation time: about 50 minutes

Seed Vinaigrette (recipe follows)

5 large red thin-skinned potatoes, scrubbed

1 cup thinly sliced celery

1/2 cup thinly sliced green onions

1 small red bell pepper, seeded and finely chopped

Salt

1 Prepare Seed Vinaigrette and set aside.

2 Place unpeeled potatoes in a 5- to 6-quart pan and add enough water to cover. Bring to a boil over high heat; then reduce heat, partially cover, and boil gently until potatoes are tender when pierced (25 to 30 minutes). Drain, immerse in cold water until cool, and drain again. Cut into 3/4-inch cubes.

3 In a large bowl, gently mix potatoes, celery, onions, bell pepper, and Seed Vinaigrette. Season to taste with salt. If made ahead, cover and refrigerate for up to 1 day. Serve cold or at room temperature.

makes 6 to 8 servings

SEED VINAIGRETTE

In a wide frying pan, combine 1 teaspoon each mustard seeds, cumin seeds, and fennel seeds. Cook over medium heat until fragrant (3 to 5 minutes), stirring often. Using the back of a heavy spoon, coarsely crush seeds. Remove from heat and mix in 2 tablespoons salad oil, 1/3 cider vinegar, 1/2 teaspoon coarsely ground pepper, and 1 clove garlic (minced or pressed).

per serving: 169 calories, 3 g protein, 30 g carbohydrates, 4 g total fat, 0 mg cholesterol, 29 mg sodium

sweet potato & apple salad

preparation time: about 1 hour
cooling time: about 30 minutes

2 pounds small sweet potatoes or yams

1/2 cup walnuts

2 tablespoons honey

1 teaspoon grated lemon peel

1 tablespoon lemon juice

3/4 teaspoon ground ginger

1/2 teaspoon ground cinnamon

1 cup plain nonfat yogurt

2 large red-skinned apples, cored and cut into 3/4-inch cubes

3/4 cup thinly sliced celery

Salt

1 Place unpeeled potatoes in a 5- to 6-quart pan and add enough water to cover. Bring to a boil over high heat; then reduce heat, partially cover, and boil gently until potatoes are tender when pierced (25 to 30 minutes). Drain and let stand until cool (about 30 minutes). Meanwhile, toast walnuts in a wide frying pan over medium-high heat until lightly browned and fragrant (about 3 minutes), stirring often. Pour out of pan and let cool.

2 In a large bowl, stir together honey, lemon peel, lemon juice, ginger, cinnamon, and yogurt. Peel potatoes and cut into 3/4-inch cubes; then add potatoes, apples, celery, and 1/3 cup of the walnuts to dressing in bowl. Mix gently. Season to taste with salt. Transfer to a serving bowl and garnish with remaining walnuts.

makes 8 to 10 servings

per serving: 207 calories, 4 g protein, 39 g carbohydrates, 5 g total fat, 0.5 mg cholesterol, 42 mg sodium

black bean, corn & pepper salad

preparation time: about 15 minutes
chilling time: at least 1 hour

2 cans (about 15 oz. *each*) black beans or cannellini (white kidney beans), drained and rinsed; or 4 cups cooked black beans or cannellini, drained and rinsed

1 ½ cups cooked fresh yellow or white corn kernels (from 2 medium-size ears corn); or 1 package (about 10 oz.) frozen corn kernels, thawed

1 large red bell pepper, seeded and finely chopped

2 small fresh jalapeño chiles, seeded and finely chopped

½ cup firmly packed chopped cilantro

¼ cup lime juice

2 tablespoons salad oil

Salt and pepper

Lettuce leaves, rinsed and crisped

1 In a large bowl, combine beans, corn, bell pepper, chiles, cilantro, lime juice, and oil; mix lightly. Season to taste with salt and pepper. Cover and refrigerate for at least 1 hour or for up to 1 day.

2 To serve, line a serving bowl with lettuce leaves; spoon in bean mixture.

makes 6 servings

per serving: 197 calories, 9 g protein, 29 g carbohydrates, 6 g total fat, 0 mg cholesterol, 186 mg sodium

orzo with spinach & pine nuts

preparation time: about 35 minutes

8 ounces dry orzo or tiny shell-shaped pasta

2 tablespoons pine nuts

1 tablespoon olive oil

½ cup minced red onion

4 ounces stemmed spinach leaves, rinsed and chopped

2 medium-size pear-shaped (Roma-type) tomatoes, seeded and diced

3 ounces feta cheese, crumbled

¼ cup chopped parsley

Pepper

1 In a 5- to 6-quart pan, cook orzo in about 3 quarts boiling water until just tender to bite (about 5 minutes); or cook according to package directions. Drain, rinse with cold water until cool, and drain again.

2 Toast pine nuts in a medium-size frying pan over medium heat until golden (3 to 5 minutes), stirring often. Pour out of pan and set aside.

3 Heat oil in pan. Add onion; cook, stirring often, until soft (about 5 minutes). Add spinach and cook, stirring, just until wilted (about 2 more minutes).

4 In a large bowl, gently mix pasta, pine nuts, and spinach mixture. Add tomatoes, cheese, and parsley. Mix again; season to taste with pepper. If made ahead, cover and refrigerate for up to 4 hours. Serve at room temperature.

makes 6 servings

per serving: 229 calories, 9 g protein, 32 g carbohydrates, 8 g total fat, 13 mg cholesterol, 181 mg sodium

index